THE JUGGLING ACT

Working mothers share their experiences

THE JUGGLING ACT

Working mothers share their experiences

ADRIENNE KATZ

BLOOMSBURY

First published 1992 by Bloomsbury Publishing Limited,
2 Soho Square, London W1V 5DE

Copyright © 1992 by Adrienne Katz

The moral right of the author has been asserted

A CIP record for this book is available from the British Library

ISBN 0 7475 0656 6

Designed by Geoff Green
Typeset by Hewer Text Composition Services, Edinburgh
Printed by Clays Ltd, St Ives plc

Contents

Part Five – Life choices

Foreword

'Women who seek equality with men lack ambition.'

The anonymous author of this piece of graffiti scrawled on a wall in a women's toilet cannot have known how her words would echo in my mind. In the discussions with women that inform this book I found shared criticism of our male-oriented society. Women are now rethinking what we might aim for in the future and realising that, rather than mimic the masculine mode, we might be able to mould patriarchal society around our feminine curves.

Yes, women do have different value systems – they are concerned with what they consider to be the important things: their relationships with others, their emotional well-being and worries about how their work life affects those close to them. These concerns are not weaknesses – they are strengths. Wearing 'cultural masks' at work in order to succeed in the male way denies these strengths.

These valuable gifts exist widely, they are not rare among women. Joining the rat-race, excelling in a high-powered career is exciting and satisfying on one level, but it is not in itself enough for many women. They question whether this ladder-like career pattern is a desirable way of life even for men, let alone women. Overwhelmingly, women want to make a contribution in the workplace, to be treated on equal terms within it and fulfil their potential, and at the same time they want their right to motherhood, family life and emotional fulfilment. Too often women are still being forced to make choices.

Women have arrived at equality in many areas, although they are still denied it in others. For many working mothers this has meant walking an unmapped road. But already there are those who are signalling that they don't like what they see when they get there. Aping the male pattern will not do for women – they want something better. When the hand that rocks the cradle also wields a scalpel or runs a business, another mother comes face-to-face with the tensions of working and mothering. There is the rigidity of the standard working day and working week, and the segregation of home and work. There are school hours that do not harmonise with work hours, and problems with childcare. And then there are other people's attitudes.

There is little in the way our workplaces view our out of work responsibilities that acknowledges the importance of the family. Britain has the highest number of working women in Europe but one of the worst publicly-funded childcare programmes. The issue is wider, however, than simply providing childcare – which, of course, is a must: it is how to bring about a balanced way of life in which we can work and parent, and, later, take care of the elderly.

Women's goal seems to be changing. No longer are they simply seeking equality; now women are talking of a new vision of society in which their influence can bring about a greater balance between work and home life for both women and men.

This may be a more successful way of living for all of us. Our relationships with others could be valued more highly than self-interest. As parents we could band together to cause a shift in thinking. By placing children and their care in a more central position – no longer the preserve of the mother alone, tucked away in the privacy of the home – they would become the responsibility of mothers and fathers helped by the community as a whole. The wellbeing of our children is not a private women's problem, it is vital to the future of the country. With peace of mind, knowing that their children's welfare rates high on the scale, women will be freer to make a greater contribution in the workplace.

The next phase could be one in which we fully understand the important rôle human resources play in improving both our economic resources and quality of life. This is no race to the finish between men and women – we need to navigate the obstacles hand in hand, supported by the state.

Adrienne Katz

Acknowledgements

This book is the result of women sharing their lives with me. Many contributors are mentioned by name, or, when I was asked, by pseudonym. Hundreds more are anonymous, but I took in what you told me in chance meetings, in letters and phone calls, surveys, questionnaires and interviews. Without all of you it would not have been possible. I am grateful not only for the information you gave me but for the warmth and friendship I found at every turn. The experience of being in touch with and helped by women up and down the country is one which I shall never forget.

I want to thank Deborah Owen for her unwavering faith in the project over two years, and, with her, Judi Dooling and Rosemary Scoular for dealing with my day-to-day worries. Thank you to Liane Katz for her vital computer work, remarkable patience and support. To Diana Craig for her valuable editing, to Ian Katz for reading the manuscript and coming up with lunch, constructive criticism, encouragement and flowers when most needed, Nomi Rowe for reading and words of wisdom, Helene Gonski for keeping me in touch with Australia via cuttings and books, Hazel Gevint who got drafted in for research while on her holiday and the staff of Bloomsbury for their contribution.

To the many friends and contacts in the USA, thank you for the deluge of material.

To John Katz for coping with my obsession and the loss of a dining room for two years, my thanks.

To *Good Housekeeping* magazine, who received a huge response to their survey and kindly allowed me access to the replies. This enabled me to contact women across the country and in all walks of life.

To Mary Adams at Nottingham University, Dilys Daws at

the Child Psychotherapy Trust, Irene Pilia and her daughter at Working Mothers Association, Childcare Now, Sue Slipman of the National Council for One Parent Families and Suzanne Viner of the Advertising Archive, thank you for your assistance.

To the many organisations whose information or press officers helped me – many thanks.

The author acknowledges a debt to Fidelis Morgan's *A Misogynist's Sourcebook*.

Part One

Mummy, who are you?

'Whatever else motherhood is, it is not something which you take on or do on top of everything else, it seems to alter every layer of one's being therefore once embarked upon cannot be completely discarded.'

Hilary Land, 'Girls Can't Be Professors, Mummy', in *Balancing Acts: On Being a Mother*, ed. Catherine Gieve (1989)

'Always in all ways
A mother shows her love'

'To a perfect mum, a
perfect day'

'Mother, I just don't know how you manage to be so wonderful
all the time. . . . Always putting others before yourself.
Always remembering to do thoughtful things
Always managing to find a smile
Loving just seems to come naturally to you.
I want you to know how special you are to me
And that I wish you the happiest birthday ever.'

'There's beauty in the special way
A mother gently fills each day
With love.'

'A mother is someone
Who shows loving care
By taking the time
To be always there.'

'It's just your way to be there
When we need a helping hand,
To take the time to show us
That you care and understand
It's just your way to add a touch
Of joy to every day.'

'Mum, what would I do without you? Starve.'

Lines from greeting cards reflecting society's perception
of what a mother should be.

Images of motherhood

'I want a girl, just like the girl that married dear old dad.'
Song by William Dillon, 1911

Earth mother or engineer, madonna or managing director – can we successfully superimpose these new images upon the age-old view of motherhood? Little Johnny, growing up in the late twentieth century, might well proudly state, 'My mum's a policewoman,' but just how much has motherhood changed, when the very idea of 'mother' and what she stands for has been shaped in the Western mind for centuries by images in art and literature? More recently, and most powerfully, it has also been projected in advertising, films and the media.

Despite paying lip service to equal opportunities for women in all walks of life, we are unconsciously affected by the images of motherhood that portray the beauty of the self-sacrificing ideal and the special love between mother and child. This has led people to believe that it is impossible to be a 'complete' mother and hold down paid work outside the home. Perhaps this is the source of much of the criticism working mothers find themselves receiving.

A mother and child are seen to form the essential family unit, the eternal icon. For so long women have defined themselves through their ability to become mothers; it is a relatively new and startling idea that they might define themselves in terms of being a policewoman, too. With mothers out in the workplace, do we any longer really know who 'Mummy' is? She does not conform to any stereotype: the age-old conventions have been shattered. She may still be the central, loving figure in her child's life, but she can be a solicitor, or a supermarket cashier too.

The power of advertising

In the post-war rebuilding of Britain, women were given a new
enemy to fight – dirt and germs. The war on dirt was waged
with new appliances and cleaning fluids. Advertisements showed
women being judged by the outside world according to how white
their sheets and shirts were or how sparkling their floors. In early
TV ads, nosy neighbours are shown dropping in and telling the
housewife how to 'wash whiter'. The image of a good mother
was projected as measurable in terms of how her family looked:
keeping up appearances took on a new meaning. Mum is always
shown inside the home, while her family are seen setting off or
coming back from a day 'out there', fortified by her good breakfast
or accompanied by a protective shield of love in the form of a
sparkling white shirt.

A 1950s Persil advertisement put it thus: 'This woman is alone,
yet not alone. Even though her family may be apart *from* her they
are still a part *of* her, being judged by the care she takes of them,
being judged by how clean and white she keeps their clothes, just
as she is being judged by that same whiteness. Persil is part of
her strength and their happiness. As a wife, as a mother, she uses
Persil.'

With all this repetition of the word 'judge', the poor Mrs Average
Housewife found herself feeling nervous and guilty lest she be found
wanting. She feared other women as competitors. Being a wife and
mother was depicted as a career, and homemaking skills were
revered.

Kelloggs cornflakes laid on the guilt with a heavy hand: 'This is
how his wife sent him off to work this morning. Good job she didn't
see him two hours later. It's his wife's fault probably – he's had
nothing since supper, twelve hours ago. [Hubby is shown getting
into trouble at work for not completing a schedule.] No proper
breakfast. He said he hadn't time. Before his toast and tea give
him a good big plate of cornflakes – delicious. [Hubby is shown
doing "a good day's work" and saying to his secretary, "Remind me
to take home a bunch of flowers for my wife."]

A woman received accolades if she treated her man a little like
a child. She was guardian of health and hearth and morals too.
Generations of women have been made to believe this propaganda.
To be a proper wife and mother is to be skilled at cleaning,
laundering and baking; sitting quietly, talking problems through,

or being understanding, stimulating or fun to be with are activities never referred to. At the end of the day, what will a child remember most – a sparkling floor or the good times together?

How clean is clean?

Housekeeping: The care and maintenance of a home includes: (1) providing sufficient and suitable food for all members of the household; (2) care and cleaning of the house, its equipment and furnishings; (3) care and cleaning of the clothing of the household members; (4) personal care of members of the family, including care of children and invalids; (5) responsibility for heating and lighting the house and sometimes for its repair; (6) control of household expenditures; (7) engaging and supervising household employees; (8) purchasing food, supplies, equipment, furnishings and clothings; (9) maintaining relations with other families and with organisations in the community; (10) taking part in and sponsoring such activities of the community as garbage disposal, water supply, good markets inspection, street cleaning, smoke and dust elimination, or any community housekeeping projects which have a bearing on personal housekeeping problems; and (11) making suitable provision for the comfort of the family members and guests. Housekeeping is one of the most comprehensive occupations that a woman can undertake.

Encyclopaedia Britannica, 1961

As new gadgets and cleansers were developed to make housework easier, standards ironically became higher. Advertising had to create new anxieties for mothers in order to persuade them to buy more products. It was not enough for the home to be clean – it had to smell nice too. Whiteness, as an extra dimension of cleanness, was another new concept. More time – and more products – were needed to get things 'whiter than white', 'dazzling' or 'sunshine white'. 'Just clean isn't good enough for me' ran an ad for Bold washing powder.

Great emphasis was also put on germs that you could not see. Invisible germs lurked, breeding and multiplying, ready to attack her family if the housewife did not kill them first. When in these Fifties' and Sixties' TV ads, the housewife succeeded in her war against germs, some male figure would frequently be heard to say 'Clever girl!' in a patronising way. As a BBC programme on advertising explained: 'Toilets rather than beaches became that unguarded entry into all we hold dear.'

Mother love

Today, ads no longer show housework as the main way in which women get satisfaction and praise. Oxo created a couple, Katy and

Philip, whose story developed through years of Oxo commercials and three different Philips. Nowadays Katy is permitted a life of her own – as long as she makes the dinner first. She is shown coming home late on Tuesday night. The family have come in and eaten the delicious casserole she has left for them in the oven, a symbol of her maternal love. Husband and children have not left her a mouthful. This is successful mothering.

Products now promise freedom and convenience but are always aimed at mother – for it is she who will buy the product and see to the chores. As demands on women grew during the Eighties, women found that, to be a good mother and work outside the home, something had to give and most of my interviewees said that after personal time for hobbies or friends, it was housework.

This seldom happens without some sense of guilt, though. There are tasks undone, standards not met, particularly if mother or mother-in-law is around to draw attention to these earlier values. In addition to having to achieve at work, women are retaining the demands to achieve at home, putting themselves into an intensely stressful situation: only Superwoman could handle all aspects of this striving.

Motherhood in art

'I consider that women who are authors, lawyers, and politicians are monsters.'

Pierre Auguste Renoir, 1841–1919

Images of mothers in art bring gentle Madonnas to mind, and conjure up the admired ideal, selfless, chaste and ever-loving. This is the view so often created by male artists idolising motherhood as women's highest calling and purest achievement. It has become an icon representing a sacred bond between mother and child which is instinctive and admits no irritation, exhaustion, anger or frustration – which any real live harassed mum will tell you come as part of the package. The cherubic child in these pictures could not possibly throw his porridge on the floor or sick up sour-smelling milk. Lusciously naked, his soft plump body is always shown without nappies (or the equivalent in Renaissance times), the mundane necessary changing of which brings a real mum down to earth.

Earlier images of mothers are found in primitive cultures where female goddesses and fertility figures are found as powerful life-givers. Abundant, fecund and rooted in the natural world, these

sculptures are echoed in our time by Henry Moore's large mother
figures and Picasso's mammoth mothers. Helen Kay, author of
Picasso's World of Children, explains the artist's depiction of mothers.
Picasso 'sees as the child sees: the world is the mother and the
mother is the world. In the beginning the boundaries are the
mother's arms. They make a unity – an island.'

Modern mothers can feel an empathy with these capable, rock-like
figures offering total protection and support to the child figure.
Women *are* capable and supportive and giving. They frequently
become the rock on which the family unit depends. But look again
– these mothers, particularly Moore's, are faceless and featureless,
their individual identity submerged in the act of mothering, which
seems to blot out personality. Perhaps this is what so many modern
mothers fear. They fear becoming featureless, eternal mother figures
with no identity, sexuality or independence. Journalist, writer and
broadcaster, Anne Karpf, became aware of this change when she
became a mother: 'I'm so unused to the invisibility of a woman
with a pram, I was pushing the pram the other day and I saw
some man walk past and it was just the way that he . . . didn't
acknowledge my existence.'

Sheila McGregor of the Fine Art Department at Birmingham
Art Gallery argues that the majority of these classic images were
made by men who overwhelmingly endorse the sexual status quo,
implying a biologically ordained division of sexual labour which
has been perpetuated by a patriarchal society. She believes that
the cumulative impact of these images has built up our view
of motherhood in Western consciousness, endlessly affirming the
importance of motherhood as woman's most valuable contribution
to the shaping of human society.

'Yes, but . . .' women are saying. We want to keep our mothering
power, but it need not take away our sense of self. We need not define
ourselves only as reproduction machines. We can bring to our
mothering a new element – experience of the outside world. This
can add, rather than subtract, to what we offer our children.

The rôle and responsibilities of the mother have changed
and taken a new form. That traditional rock-like support that we
were once expected to provide from within the home we may now
provide from outside it, by going out into the world to become
the breadwinners and providers for our families. Within the home
itself, we no longer lift and heave heavy buckets of water on to
a stove to heat for washing, we no longer need to spend many

hours preserving food or baking. We can bung the washing in the machine, buy a loaf of bread and fresh or tinned fruit any day we need it. So what are we to do with the energy and time that we now have free of housework? What shall we make of the years after our children have grown?

Clare Charnley, in a contemporary artists exhibition on the theme 'mothers', produced a work of metaphor that echoed precisely what so many are saying about motherhood in the 1990s. Entitled *Dropping eggs*, the work shows a woman's hands holding hen's eggs to her body, successfully holding several, but at the same time more than she can possibly hold drop past her, presumably to fall and smash. There is clearly an impossibility about this task. Some eggs elude her grasp, some hover within reach – if she were to grab these, the ones she now holds would fall. The egg is the perfect image here as a symbol of life, delicate yet carrying such potential – and yet overriding all the fragility, vulnerability and tenderness implicit in the work is the power and strength of the woman's hands. This one picture seems to sum up motherhood now.

A moment in history

'Women who work are much more likely to wander than those who don't.'

Piers Paul Read, 1983

Any woman born this century can point to striking transformations in women's lives during her lifetime. Chameleon-like, she has been expected to change and match up to the prevailing dramatic shifts in peace or war. These shifts mainly concern her rôle as mother or worker.

At one moment, it is expected that she works for the good of the country, or to support her family; at another, she is told that her children will suffer irreparable harm if she is not with them every day of the year. She is told to fulfil her potential by going out to work, or blamed, when she does so, for delinquency, eating disorders, homosexuality, schizophrenia and truancy in her children. As recently as 1990, an article appeared in the press saying that today's delinquents must be the result of their mothers' working.

For a thinking woman of today, the two sides of the working/mothering argument are still alive. We are in one of the extremes of the pendulum swing as it points towards 'worker', but we cannot ignore the issues at the other extreme of the swing. It is as mothers, not workers, that we are judged, and judged harshly: 'She's not much of a mother, leaving those children like that,' we hear.

Mothers of dependent children are working outside the home in greater numbers than ever before in peacetime. It is also true that the relationship between a mother and her child needs to be built up to become intimate, continuous and reliable. How then does a woman both work and mother? Perhaps the solution to this complex question is to come in this decade, a time when mothers are urgently needed in the workforce, and can thus demand a fairer system in the workplace with recognition of their rights both as workers and mothers.

Might the pendulum swing come to rest in the centre? Might we back away from extremes? The idea that a child will thrive simply because his mother is with him constantly is as extreme as the belief that she should keep him at a distance for 'there are rocks ahead for the overkissed child', as J.B. Watson believed. Can we balance the equation with effective mothering on the one hand and contributing at work on the other?

A welcome in the workplace?

Where have we got to in the story of women at work this century? We need to see ourselves as part of a greater pattern. Each working woman is a link in the chain. Our individual problems are not unique but belong to a wider group. Our beliefs and behaviour are shaped by the moment in history which we represent. Until it is comfortable and possible for parents of both sexes to work and parent with the children's needs fully recognised, the story will not have a satisfactory end.

There has been no steady ladder-like progression for women's acceptance in the workplace, rather a series of leaps forward and slides or switchbacks turning the clock back. Prevailing powerful attitudes to women's rôle have influenced our own perception of it. Fashions in childcare have come and gone. Babies have been labelled by the childcare expert popular at the time, so we've had Truby King babies or Spock babies, who have been left to cry or hastily picked up, forced into routines or demand-fed.

Turning points

'I am constantly appalled by the strident voices of women claiming equality with men.'

Professor Northcote Parkinson, 1909–88

The needs of the country for workers, and the shifts in the population caused by the terrible death rate of World War I, all had a direct effect on the way women were to mother and take their place in society.

The two World Wars were to be landmarks. World War I resulted in women getting suffrage and the Sex Disqualification (Removal) Act of 1919. This Act allowed women (in theory) to 'assume or carry on any civil profession or vocation'. Many areas of work were not covered by the Act, for example synods of the Church of England and the Stock Exchange, but it was a landmark in women's progress. World War II was followed by the Education Act of 1944, the Family Allowance and the beginnings of a move towards equal pay. The Education Act provided compulsory and free secondary education for all. Girls could no longer be taken out of school by parents to mind siblings or to go to work. Bright students could take the Eleven Plus exam and the grammar school route to university. The alternative to grammar schools were secondary moderns, and there were complaints that these trained girls for second class futures. However there was a new equality of opportunity and a belief in the importance of education. Many women I interviewed were the first in their family to go to university as a result of this. Schooling was compulsory up to age 15, making children dependent on parents for longer. Girls' private schools were unaffected.

Since the mid-nineteenth century, the idea that women were uniquely and morally qualified for childrearing, and to be the guardians of the home, reigned unchallenged. Married women and mothers were ideologically expected to devote themselves to home and family. Of course, this went hand-in-hand with the concept of the male breadwinner and assumed there would always be enough of these to go round.

This overriding view of women's rôle was powerful, yet cast aside when necessary. Attitudes to women in the workplace have always been expedient. During World War I, women rallied to take on jobs in munitions and as V.A.D.s, and to work on the land when needed. Despite the jeers that initially greeted the idea of women on the land, these girls were to raise the status of rural women. The War Committee on Women in Industry (appointed two months before the end of the war) even went so far as to suggest equal pay for equal work, but this potentially progressive move was abruptly aborted. It was to be debated until 1970.

Back to the kitchen

'The wave of feminism which swept Britain after 1918 caused widespread unemployment, a general trade depression, and an alarming decline in our birthrate . . . As soon as Hitlerism has

been defeated the combined forces of the various men's organisations
will launch their campaign against a menace just as threatening to
Britain as Hitlerism – Feminism.'

From a leaflet distributed during World War II
by the National Men's Defence League,
a British servicemen's association, c1942

Suddenly, with the war over, it was thought wrong for a woman to
occupy a job that was rightfully a man's. 'But now the masquerade
was over,' writes Ruth Adam in *A Woman's Place*, 'it was time to
hang up the doublet and hose behind the kitchen door and get
back to skirts and aprons.'

Women's aspirations were expected to take a nosedive into banal
housewifery. Men were discharged at a rate of 10,000 a day for
six months. The boom in industry and the weak way in which
women stepped down were to create the jobs the men needed.
Adam describes how employers did not want to let the women
go. They had worked well and had proved 'easy to manage, docile
and cheap. The working world slid back into the old conventions
of female jobs and male jobs.'

By this time, women had also begun to make headway in the
professions. But despite the exceptional work they had done during
the war in the field of medicine, medical schools now closed most
doors to women trainees. Teachers accepted lower pay than male
teachers, though the work was the same. Lawyers did better as so
many male members of the profession had been lost that daughters
were welcomed into family practices.

Spinster teachers were examples of women dedicated to and
fulfilled by their careers. After nurses, they represented the second
largest women's profession. They exerted a strong influence on the
aspirations of those bright, educated young women who realised
that they might not necessarily expect to find a man to support
them. On marrying, however, teachers were expected to resign. The
idea that a woman could devote herself unstintingly to her job while
bringing up a family was still unacceptable (until, in 1942, a circular
published by the Department of Education and Science stated that
it was not right to debar women because of marriage).

The Depression

'It will upset the applecart if women get equal pay.'

Union official at Vauxhall Motors, Luton, 1977

By early 1920, any talk of equal pay had begun to recede and unemployment loomed. Women realised they were going to be lucky to keep any kind of job a man could do, and it might well be the fact that a woman cost her employer less that was the deciding factor in keeping her on.

The appearance of the Bright Young Things was a short-lived reaction to the lack of young men. The Bright Young Things described a fashionable group of women in a phase between the wars during which younger women were determinedly 'modern' in fashion and behaviour. They showed a marked contrast in attitude to the prevailing views of their parents. They wore tomboyish haircuts, flatchested fashions and had boyish nicknames. They considered themselves sexually liberated. Their attempts to take jobs were frustrated as during the Depression more jobs began to be reserved for men, and woman found doors closing for them once more.

As the Depression wore on, resentment grew against those women who were working, as they were seen as clinging limpet-like to jobs ex-soldiers might have done. There was also a suggestion that they worked for pin money, taking jobs from male breadwinners. In fact, a large number of these working women were supporting dependants, without the help of a man, in the decimated post-war population.

Working class women, too, found themselves supporting the family as their men were increasingly out of work. Women could go into domestic service and take repetitive factory jobs as well as work in the mills. This led to a diminution of the man's authority within the home as he was no longer the breadwinner before whom all must show respect. Images of capable women struggling to keep their family above the breadline are typical of this period.

Another war

For a second time, war was to have an effect on the numbers of women at work. Children were placed in state-provided nurseries and mothers were required to work. Conscription into war work touched almost everyone. In 1943, nine out of 10 single women and four out of five married women, between the ages of 18 and 40, were in the services or in industry. During the Depression and the two wars, women did not have to face a dilemma over whether to work or to stay home with the children. Working mothers felt that they were contributing to the good of the family and society as a whole. There was a certainty for them. They did not work for personal satisfaction, for interest, pin money, to get out of the home or for personal identity. They did not feel guilty about working. 'Women's work was valuable then. The war effort depended on us women,' says Stella Phillips, whose child was in a nursery at the time.

Going out to work, however, did allow women to enjoy an excitement and companionship they did not find inside the home. Once having tasted this, there were many who knew it was what they wanted.

The cult of motherhood

History since the war has telescoped the ups and downs of women's lives into a fast roller coaster ride, and changes for women have swung from one extreme to another.

After World War II, the pendulum was to swing abruptly away from wartime ideas, bringing the needs of the child to the fore. This post-war backlash was to characterise our ideas on the family through the decades to follow.

In the Fifties, in contrast to the earlier acceptance of working women, the child's needs were presented as paramount. Women were urged to stay at home and be with their children 365 days a year for fear of causing maternal deprivation. As psychological theories were popularised and childcare manuals became widely available, mothers were held responsible if children were deprived or disturbed. These manuals were written by paediatricians and pyschologists spreading the ideas of Sigmund Freud, Melanie Klein and John Bowlby. In their writing, they made childcare less a matter of instinct and family lore than a professional skill.

Understanding maternal deprivation

'Mother love is as important for mental health as vitamins and proteins are for physical health.'

John Bowlby

Psychological studies focused on the damage maternal deprivation caused children in institutions (there were 100,000 wards of the community living in appalling conditions at the end of the war). The work undertaken by John Bowlby became universally accepted as the watchword in the field of childcare. Published initially as a World Health Organisation monograph, *Maternal Care and Mental*

Health, it came out as a popular paperback, *Childcare and the Growth of Love*, gaining widespread acceptance. The bond between mother and child was shown to be essential to the child's emotional wellbeing. This work helped change attitudes in hospitals towards sick children and their parents, who are now encouraged to stay with very young children.

The work of Lady Allen, president of the World Organisation for Early Childhood Education, also contributed to the argument. In a pamphlet called *Whose Children?*, she revealed some of the appalling cruelty she had seen in the treatment of children in institutions. Force feeding and cruel punishments were the norm. A wave of public anger greeted these revelations. Almost as though people felt guilty at the neglect of children during the war years, there was now an orgy of child-centred ideas. Conscientious mothers absorbed the new theories and became afraid to leave their children at all, especially if they were under three years old.

Family is everything

Voices in government and the media also joined the chorus of experts now telling mothers how to mother. Giving centre stage to the importance of the family was in fact an intentional attempt at restructuring post-war Britain, an attempt at reconciliation, at creating stability after chaos and at redressing the imbalance necessitated in home lives during the war. Family was all, the ideology stated. It was 'the comforting sameness of its image replicated a million times across the barriers of wealth and class,' wrote Liz Heron, 'that can transcend and overwhelm the significance of the other structures and institutions in which ordinary lives are caught.'

The new domesticity

Wife wanted:
Must be able to
Look like an Angel
Cook like a gourmet
And bonk like a rabbit.
From a T-shirt, 1988 (Attitudes haven't changed much!)

A girl who had worked in factories during the war, clocking on in the cold mornings, was now encouraged to stay home and make a comfortable nest with a husband, a baby and the new mod cons. Now she could aspire to owning a fridge, a vacuum cleaner and a washing machine, and even a television set on which more material goods could be temptingly displayed.

This was a time when 'respectable mothers' did not go to work: it was simply 'not done'. 'My mother did not work, wives of army officers simply did not work,' said Dyann, describing her Fifties childhood. 'My mother used her brains and abilities in charity drives and bridge games,' remembers Benita. Prosperity meant that the male breadwinner could bring in enough for the family, and it rather implied he was not managing this if his wife went to work. The death rate in World War II had not decimated the male population quite as much as in the first war, so there was not the same percentage of single women heads of households. New housing estates blossomed in the suburbs and women were able to enjoy the benefits of electricity and hot and cold running water, but found themselves rather lonely and often isolated. Modern furniture beckoned, better methods of cleaning were joined by an emphasis on laundering and hygiene, and lessons on etiquette were given in women's magazines. There could be no doubt about what was 'done' or 'not done', and the right way to do it. Above all, the care of husband and children in terms of physical and mental health was thrust forward as the pressing preoccupation of the Fifties.

In this intense desire to see women stay home, there was an element of political manipulation, as the thousands of women who had done war work were now to be wished away and the nurseries closed. Rather than have a huge, discontented, unemployed female population, it was deemed better for the nation to urge them to stay home. And in this the state was aided by burgeoning industries finding a market for household appliances and products. Manufacturers advertised furiously to create an image of full-time housework and germ-killing being the way to protect your loved ones.

At the same time, ironically, soaring divorce figures, a high illegitimate birthrate and greater social mobility and class movement put the family under threat as never before. (In 1954 it was estimated that one marriage in 15 would end in divorce, compared with one in 60 in 1937 and one in 500 in 1911.)

Baby boom

'There'll be love and laughter, and peace ever after . . .' was the song on everyone's lips as 401,210 couples began married life together after the war ended. The year 1947 saw the birthrate soar. The babies born then were to grow up in a new climate, a post-war fever of optimism in which people believed a new society would be created. These toddlers thrived on milk and orange juice, cod liver oil and NHS care, and with them they took on a bold new confidence as Liz Heron describes in her introduction to an account of growing up in the Fifties, *Truth, Dare or Promise*: 'Along with the orange juice, the cod liver oil, the malt supplement and the free school milk, we may also have absorbed a sense of our own worth . . . as if history were on our side.'

Now, in the 1990s, girls born in the baby boom are around as a significantly large group of working mothers who grew up at a time when ideas on mothering were the opposite of today's. These working mothers are characterised by feelings of guilt, uncertainty and doubt. The cult of motherhood in the Fifties, that was so much a part of their childhood, clashes with the realities of life in the Nineties. Part of a transitional generation caught between two value systems, these women seem to agonise over much of what they are doing, far more than the wartime worker or even today's younger woman. As they grew, many new influences would have a bearing on the changing aspirations of these baby-boom girls.

Education for all

'The chief distinction in the intellectual powers of the two sexes is shewn by man attaining to higher eminence, in whatever he takes up, than woman can attain – whether requiring deep thought, reason, or imagination, or merely the uses of the senses and hands.'

Charles Darwin, 1809–82

One very important influence was the 1944 Education Act, under which it was compulsory to stay on at school till 15. Parents could not argue that they would not spend money on a daughter's education, or keep her home because she was needed to look after little siblings. Girls took and passed the Eleven Plus examination – a passport to further education – and many found themselves the first in their families to go to university.

Sue Slipman was one of these girls. Her mother had worked as a shop assistant and in a pie and mash shop with her husband. Leaving school after 'O' levels, 'it was expected I would do a secretarial course,' Sue says. 'After a week I went demented.' Fortunately a teacher took Sue aside and said she should do 'A' levels and go to university. 'It came as a shock that I might go. No one in my family had ever been to university and the expectation was that everyone worked at the minimum leaving age.' Sue today heads the National Council for One Parent Families.

The teenagers

The transitional generation also saw the rise of a new phenomenon – the teenager. Providing the perfect market for the fashion and music industries because of the prosperity of the times and their disposable income, they rocked and rolled, they experimented with their appearance, with sex and lifestyles. They bucked the establishment. Growing up in the Sixties with rock, folk song and jazz mixing with protest songs in their ears, they wore their hair long, their miniskirts short and heard the first stirrings of the women's movement. Powerful and conflicting images swirled around them – bra-burning man haters, chicks who faithfully hero-worshipped their men, earth-mother types who baked wholemeal bread and imbued childrearing with spiritual qualities, and career girls competing with men in the marketplace. What should these teenagers become? Anything seemed possible and experimenting was permitted. 'We were caught in a warp of sexist history: too feminist to make our own clothes, too feminine to knock up our own bookshelves,' writes Australian columnist Anna Maria Dell'Oso.

Women's lib

The women's movement that grew during this time promised equality with men and brought dissatisfaction in its wake as 'consciousness was raised'. Young women reached for the promise of a career at the exclusion of a private life: not for them the subjugation of housewifery their mothers knew, they thought at 20. But at 38 or so, with the biological clock ticking away, many were to find that, in the 1980s, they wanted to have a child. The choice still seemed to be as stark as when they were 20 – marriage and kids, or career. They talk of how it seemed to be either one or the other: 'I think it's to do with the whole thing in the family of my sister being given the role of mother and me being given the role of the professional . . . it was as if neither of us was allowed to do both in some way,' Anne, journalist and late mother at 39, told me.

'The reaction of some of my feminist friends to the news that I was going to have a baby seemed to me to be one of dismay – even of letting the side down.'
Hilary Land, 'Girls Can't Be Professors, Mummy' in
Balancing Acts: On Being a Mother, ed. Catherine Gieve (1989)

I'll give up work when I marry

In the prosperity of the 'You never had it so good' years, it was generally possible for a family to live comfortably with only one breadwinner. It was not financially necessary for most wives to have jobs, so women generally expected to work only until they were married. Work for them was not a career. Finding Mr Right was still the expected route.

In later decades, however, these women found they were not content to exist in the reflected glory of spouse and children but wanted a persona of their own, and divorce statistics were to soar. Women's lib encouraged them in group sessions to strike out and assert themselves. The Pill gave them the power to choose to have children.

Finding oneself

Men, too, did not escape the effects of these changing social attitudes. All this talk about self-sufficiency for women allowed them to feel less guilty about abandoning a wife and family in search of the all-important personal fulfilment that characterised the Seventies. The needs of adults seemed to supersede those of the children. Adults were to be free to fulfil their potential – to 'find' themselves, have some 'personal space', and a proper orgasm. The 1969 Divorce Reform Act put on to the statute book ideas which were already widely held.

In 1970, the taxpayer paid £9.25 million for women who had been discarded by their men. The cult of 'Me' began to have an effect. The concept of sacrificing oneself for the children faded. The Seventies saw women surging into work for both financial and fulfilment reasons, but by the Eighties women in all walks of life found they needed to work whether or not they had been prepared for this. Two incomes were often needed to pay the mortgage in two-parent households and the rapid growth of lone-parent households left women literally holding the babies.

Equal pay

The Equal Pay Act of 1970 was to be implemented by 1975 (although there are strong arguments that this has yet to come about fully at the time of writing). The Sex Discrimination Act of 1975 was to back this up. British society had been built since the Industrial Revolution on the basis of a supporting male breadwinner, and it was difficult to adapt to the ideas of equal pay and equal opportunities. Author Ruth Adam describes it as 'like trying to conduct a Seventies lifestyle in a nineteenth-century house'.

Just a housewife

As the Seventies progressed, pressure grew on women to 'fulfil themselves in careers'. Those who admitted to being full-time housewives and mothers were made to feel dull and described as 'cabbages', vegetating. It was implied that such women were wasting their education and potential. Women's nurturing of the next generation was denigrated: it was rejected by some feminists, undervalued by society, and not felt to be a full-time occupation for the Superwoman any longer. Children's needs were to come second to the mother's need to develop a life outside the home.

This pattern was found in the USA also: 'For all the talk about the importance of children,' writes Arlie Hochschild, Professor of Sociology at Berkeley, 'the cultural climate has become subtly less hospitable to parents who put children first.' By 1984, 50 million women were working in the USA in non-domestic work full-time. Nowadays a woman of the transitional generation no longer defines herself in terms of her reproductive capability and homemaking skills: she sees herself as both breadwinner and mother. This represents a wide swing in attitude from the view in vogue in her childhood.

How old ideas linger

Despite all the economic and social change that has taken place over the past four decades, the ideal of the Fifties-style family still lingers on. Girls who grew up in the baby-boom generation were exposed to the ideal during their childhoods, and may still feel a need to aspire to it. The mothers and mothers-in-law of today who brought up their children in the Fifties may still hold on to the old view of the right way to run family life. Older men now in positions of power in government and other decision-making bodies are likely to retain this image of the family in their subconscious: the only mothering they know is the one they received.

These images of mothers in past times cling lichen-like to our subconscious. We carry all this dead wood, as expectations of what mothers should be. Some of these images are inappropriate as the gap widens between then and today's reality. It has become impossible to be a Fifties-style full-time mother and hold down a job outside the home as well. But many women are still conscientiously trying to be everything to everyone. Chameleon-like, modern woman switches rôles on the doorstep every night, tuning out work demands and tuning in to home ones.

Speaking to Lynne Barber in the *Independent*, author Muriel Spark said that she was sure '*most* men have a traditional idea of the wife's rôle. I dare say modern marriages are different, but basically there's always the woman mopping up.' This accords with the image of the ideal family presented by so many advertisements – it is the classic so-called 'cereal packet' family that consists of a father who goes out to work, a mum who stays home mopping up, and two children. In reality, in the late 1980s and early 90s, this type of family only makes up 5 per cent of families in Britain. But the power of this image of an ideal family lives on, producing guilt in many women who do not lead that life, and leading to conflicting policies at government level because the ideal does not match up to reality.

The transitional generation has experienced the extremes of the pendulum swing from the Fifties through to today. Their problems are unique for they straddle the divide between then and now. Their own attempts to mother are so different from those of their mothers. These women have had traditional mothering and home-making, and expect high standards of themselves. Yet they are the generation most changed by the Women's Movement and have experienced disapproval and discrimination to a greater extent than their daughters can imagine – as Arlene, international lawyer in the City of London, and mother of two, so succinctly puts it: 'We are the shock troops,' she says. Having known first-hand such poles of opinion and life patterns, the transitional generation may yet be the one to create a workable compromise between motherhood and career.

Mother or career woman?

'A society in which women are taught anything at all but the management of a family, the care of men and the creation of the future generation is a society which is on the way out.'

L. Ron Hubbard, founder of Scientology,
in *Questions for Our Time*, 1980

As I talked to women about our images of what a good mother is, and the sharp contrast with the real thing, one point became clear. Women believe mothering can be the towering achievement of their lives but it goes unrecognised by the world at large. This is reality, this is the real test. 'I always knew it intellectually, but now I know it emotionally – it's the hardest thing in the whole world,' says Anne, after 20 years of working and in her first year of mothering. 'Paid work is a doddle compared with this. A doddle. Paid work touches and activates all one's insecurities as well, but nothing like this. This is a killer. This really touches everything, and I have found it certainly the hardest work and most difficult challenge I've ever had. If I survive this I can climb Everest.'

In *Lifelines*, Lucy Ellman playfully suggests that 'men and now women forsake the domestic scene, not because the outside world is more important, but because fantasy is more fun than the real stuff. The blocked loo, the unironed shirts, the evening meal: these are the real unbearables. Women run from them as fast if not as successfully as men.'

In interviews with women at all stages of their lives, I asked about what happens to our mothering when we run from the nitty-gritty of the daily grind to a job more valued by the outside world. Are the attributes needed to become a good mother the antithesis of those we need to get ahead in the workplace?

Go-getter or nurturer?

At first glance it seems that a woman beating her way up a career ladder has upset the gender assumptions of active male, passive female, dominant and submissive. Perhaps that is why she is often seen as threatening to colleagues. 'Bossy', 'assertive', 'dictatorial' are words we hear describing women rising to the top, whereas of a man we are more likely to hear 'He's ambitious and has leadership qualities,' said in an admiring tone.

Conversely, we hear complaints that women are held back in work situations by their need to relate, where only performance rates praise. So, to succeed, women often emulate men and suppress their emotive qualities.

Can this assertive woman also be sensitive and responsive to her family? Our ideal of motherhood is intensely selfless, yet to get on at work a woman needs to be assertive and to have some self-preservation skills to deal with office politics and run her home. It is not easy to be earth mother and tough executive simultaneously.

The assertiveness needed at work is seen by some to be the opposite of what motherhood requires. But is this really so? It is only one facet of our masculine and feminine selves. Organising a brood of unruly kids who keep bickering needs an assertive adult leader figure certainly. Running any busy household needs the skills of a negotiator and an administrator. And yet, at the same time, you need all your awareness and sensitivity to understand and cope with a baby, the very characteristics you have to subdue at work.

Split personality

Many mothers note within themselves a work persona and a mothering one. Making the switch on the threshold each evening is the difficult bit, they say. 'It's hard,' says Danielle, a child psychoanalyst and mother. 'I think there is a tension here. I think the qualities that come out when one is trying to cope, managing, rational, plotting and assertive, and the other more quiet-paced, observant, intuitive selves come into conflict. There have been times when I've realised how horrible I've been – in terms of this domineering personality – strutting around trying to organise life.'

But the truth is that in order to cope with their dual responsibility, women find they have to be terribly efficient to survive. They start running home life like an efficiency drive. 'I think this really does affect the quality of your life,' says Danielle. When asked if women could be warned to guard against an excess of super-efficiency, she felt that they depend on these skills, and that 'it is difficult to pick it up at the time because that's your survival kit'.

Instinct or intellect?

'A beautiful woman with a brain is like a beautiful woman with a clubfoot.'

Bernard Cornfield, 1974

There is a view that the ideal mother is not using her intellect but her instinct in mothering. She intuits her child's needs and responds, whereas the intellectual fast-track mother is often described as being out-of-touch, too anxious, too full of childcare manual advice, too reliant in fact on book learning about childcare. This is a damning view and quickly quashed when you meet stimulating, intelligent and responsive mothers.

I asked Anne, a new mother in her late thirties, whether she thought intellect got in the way – a view commonly held by middle-aged childminders. 'I'm a bit uneasy with the idea that there is either intellect or you're this intuitive person,' says Anne. 'I think the reason people are less intuitive on the whole is because they don't trust their intuition. In the early weeks I did go and read everything on breastfeeding and I almost had hysterics because I was not doing it right. And I got to the stage where I'm not reading a single thing. I am trying to develop my intuition.'

Anne's reaction is typical of a new trend as working women are deprived of the company of other women in family networks and childcare groups, and have no contact with small babies. They do not encounter any babies and know almost nothing about them, so that they are seldom able to bring any experience to their new mothering rôle.

Anne admits that this is an area in which she has no experience whatsoever. 'I've reached the age of 39 having hardly met a baby at all. You feel there is no basis of confidence. But I am trying. It's true that when you're used to dealing with things in an intellectual way it calls for completely different parts of you. This method of analysing was learned over a very long period of education and growing up.'

Mothering by the book

As women surged into the workplace during the Seventies and Eighties, motherhood was not always seen as an attractive choice. It was belittling to say, 'I am just a mother.' Somewhere along the way women lost out on a body of knowledge about childcare. Scores of career-women-turned-mothers rushed to consult the professionals. In *Remaking Motherhood* Anita Shreeve writes, 'My daughter is five now, and for all of her life, I have been trying to learn how to be a mother. I pay attention to what the experts say; I compare notes with other mothers and fathers. I have a childcare library three feet long. I have had to learn to be a parent in the only way I know how – not by instinct, but by the book; not as second nature but as a career.'

There is clearly a fundamental ignorance in many educated women of basic mothering lore. Women no longer pass on a large body of childcare know-how. In the smaller modern family, girls may not see many other siblings being brought up alongside them, and may not have aunts or older sisters with children. The old extended family acted as a respository of childcare knowledge and advice, which the nuclear family sorely misses.

Feminists started out with a massive denial of the importance of nurturing which they later saw as a mistake. Their goals were competing with men on male terms and taking on male behaviour and career structure. Later a woman's right to choose to have both work and family was acknowledged. In *The Second Stage*, Betty Friedan, reflecting on the new thinking, wrote: 'Who knows what women's intelligence will contribute when it can be nourished without denying love?' If the women's movement is about first and foremost the right to be a full person, the right to selfhood, does not that right include all aspects of our nature, both caring and daring?

Although women may have begun to have a more all-embracing approach, those women who grew up in the Seventies and Eighties still find that they are strangers to nappies and teething rings. The fact that so many magazines and books give childcare advice can be seen as helpful, but that they are needed at all underlines how at all underlines how little basic knowledge parents start out with, particularly if their goals have been career-orientated.

This lack of knowledge leads, as Anne said, to loss of confidence. It may be a source of guilt and it certainly does not help the mother to be relaxed and intuitive, on her baby's wavelength, responding to the cues and signals he or she gives her. Such women have had little practice in nurturing – instead, they have been taking assertiveness courses and getting ahead in the workplace.

Respect for mothers

Women recognise that mothering is a monumental task for which they are not prepared and respected. Tina, who worked as a midwife, noticed the drop in status when she left work to bring up her baby. 'The status of bringing a child into the world is higher than childrearing,' she says.

We are in a climate in which we are urged to find our self-respect in work outside the home. When I talked to Deborah Owen, literary agent and mother of three, I asked her if she thought a woman made a better mother for having this self-respect. She replied, 'I'm darn certain of it. There is nothing worse than the doormat where the child is walking right over you.' Now, in the 1990s, we are trying to be people in our own right while at the same time being giving, loving mothers too. What we need to challenge is the assumption that our career and job skills merit greater respect than our nurturing skills. In the words of Australian columnist Anna Maria Dell'Oso, 'Now that there is no sane suggestion that women can't use their brains or men mend socks, isn't it time to ask why our society always places abstraction above the practical, caring arts anyway?'

A question of balance

Getting the balance right is so much more complex than we could ever imagine before becoming parents. How to stay emotionally available to your family while succeeding in the marketplace is the issue of our time. Women are concerned with relationships with other people in a web of intricately woven interactions. A woman will weigh up her actions and their effect on these relationships. How will promotion and longer hours affect her family? Her colleagues? Her partner? Struggling always to find a balance between work life and womanliness, career and *kinder*, she walks a tightrope between two worlds, facing daunting criticism of both her rôles.

Women have a natural reluctance to succeed at the expense of others, say the psychologists. 'It's how we react to the King of the Castle game,' says Juliana. 'Power is not an infinite commodity – if I take more you have less. What do you tell your child? Go out there and walk all over everyone? Fight? Be better than all the rest? What do you teach your child about behaviour? And what type of rôle model are you?'

Bridging the gap

Is it because our mental picture of the ideal mother is so different from the highly efficient career woman image that working mothers have borne moral disapproval and accusations of neglecting their children? Blamed for rising crime and deliquency rates, they in part believe some of this and obligingly feel guilty.

Participating in the growth and development of another human being is seen as a minor task. Men are seen as doing the important major tasks. And now women are joining them outside the home to do these, too. Children see the person taking care of them as unimportant in our culture. Her work is of little value in society. Joanne told me, 'When I was small, I didn't think my mother was frightfully important because she didn't have a job, and I used to think, gosh, I wish she was really important and had a job – I do remember that quite clearly.'

The image of motherhood needs re-thinking. There is hypocrisy in society's attitudes. On the one hand we idealise motherhood and have such high expectations of the mother, on the other child-rearing and home-making is looked down on in our culture. Children are not valued highly, and being 'just a housewife' is felt to be an embarrassing admission around a dinner party table. When will taking care of the next generation command respect, entitle parents to flexible work arrangements, and get support from state policies?

In some cultures, this conflict between work and mothering does not exist: just compare African women working in the fields, with their babies on their backs, with modern Western women, dropping their babies off en route to work and long hours apart.

Juliana has the last word: 'Women have always worked in earlier times and other societies. They have made a major contribution *and* brought up children. It's only as they try to join the structured world of commerce that men have created that it has produced this conflict with childcare.'

Part Two

Is equal opportunity
an illusion?

'They have the right to work where they want to as long
as they have dinner ready when you get home.'

John Wayne, 1907–79

---

of bringing up ha...

..ut the pressures 'ollow your instincts not your career,

thers of th **Back to work:**

olution

JUGGLING BABIES

AND BRIEFCASES

UTURE IS

The child

victims of

divorce's

HAVING BABIES AT 45 AND BEYOND

Raw deal for

sisters in law

N'T REGRET GIVING UP WORK.

MPLY THE ONLY WAY TO OFFER

4

The promise

'We were promised we could have it all, compete with men on equal terms at work and have loving happy families at home. The reality doesn't match up. We end up torn in so many directions and shouldering all the responsibility,' says Megan.

Women have been promised their share of the cake, and urged to go out to work where they could have their cake and eat it too. But the promise has not always been fulfilled. When it comes to sharing out that cake, women are still on a diet.

It was made to sound easy: 'Compete on equal terms with men in the job stakes.' What nobody admitted was that the terms were not equal. Certainly, women were educated, cared for by health services, and able to control their childbearing and, with these advantages behind them, they took off into the world of work and equal rights. But they still shouldered the bulk of the responsibility for the family within the home. A working mother is only as good as her childcare arrangements, and in the UK there is very little high-quality affordable nationwide care.

The promise was spread by women's groups, by teachers in schools and by girls themselves as they took advantage of post-war education for all and began to dream of what they might be. The Sixties saw the baby-boom generation hit university age. Large numbers of students found themselves the first in their families to go to university or stay on at school after the minimum leaving age.

Girls following on in the Seventies and Eighties have never doubted that they would work. They expect to and are educated to expect this. They seem to take for granted their hard-won rights to training and opportunities. But society has yet to acknowledge that these high numbers of women in the workplace might also have another rôle as mothers.

The Nineties have been named the decade of opportunity for women, and there are improvements in equal opportunities, in recognition of women's talents and in pay. But things are not yet equal.

New opportunities

Speaking at a March 1989 conference on work and the family, Norman Fowler, then Secretary of State for Employment, said: 'I want to see job opportunities for women increasing in the 1990s. But it is more than a matter of jobs. I want to see women have the same opportunities as men now have to build a career for themselves. . . . I believe that in 1989 we in this country are standing on the threshold of a new revolution – a revolution in employment opportunities and a revolution that will continue beyond short-term demographic upheavals. And the theme of that revolution should be not so much the Rights of Man as the Rights of Women – the right to a job in areas where men have for too long enjoyed a near monopoly; the right to flexible working conditions which will enable them to combine a job with family commitments and the right to build a career which is every bit as secure, ambitious and satisfying as the career of a man.'

Most mothers would reply that equality means having a true choice of options, and that until there is a revolution in society's attitude to the family this revolution in women's careers will be more of a nightmare than a dream.

A new vision?

Fowler touched on the need for fundamental change when he said, 'It means a change in attitude – namely that bringing up children is a shared responsibility. It is not just the responsibility of the woman. For, if that is the case, then making a career as well will be an enormous task.' Right now, in the early Nineties, making a career in the majority of households already *is* an enormous task. There is no doubt that striding forward into the world with children hanging on to your legs is doubly difficult.

Insisting on a career as the only option for women is equally constricting, however – negating women's satisfaction in nurturing a child. The Nineties are beginning to sound as claustrophobic as lacing oneself into a corset. It is as though women's choices are being narrowed rather than widened. Many want to work, and need to work. Many want to mother full time for a period but few can afford this. Most want to do both, but with better rights and conditions than exist right now.

We have been promised equality and we have now been promised New Men. What we really need is a new attitude to the family, with a flexible approach to working, enabling *both* fathers and mothers to be responsible parents.

The reality

'Society has motivated women to take part in working life, but it hasn't adjusted to catch up.'

Matz Sandman, Norwegian Minister for Children and Families, quoted in *The Guardian* (23.5.91)

So often the yawning gap between women's early goals and the reality of their lives now has come as a shock. Reality for many today is still a matter of facing a stark choice – career or children. There are successful women who have combined family with career, and they should be the rôle models of the future. There are a lucky few who earn enough to afford excellent replacement care, and are stimulated by their careers and enriched by their families. In the main, though, the common pattern is for the woman's career to go on the back burner when she has children, and then her earnings and status take a big drop when she returns to work, fitting this around her childcare obligations. High-quality, affordable, accessible childcare countrywide would be the biggest single factor in enabling women to fulfil their career hopes.

A glance at women at the top will show that by far the larger number are childless. In a survey of a thousand women who made it to the top in senior and middle management, the Guardian Royal Exchange revealed that 80 per cent were childless and only half were married. This either/or decision should have disappeared with the old marriage bar which forced women to resign when they married to devote themselves to domestic life. But there are pale echoes of it still: if your goal is to be something big in the City, or a surgeon, barrister – or, dare you think it, a judge – you will have a greater chance of getting there if you are not trailing children in your wake.

Pay and prospects

The image of the glamorous, well-paid career girl waving goodbye to her nanny and child as she dashes off to work in her Porsche is true of only a small group.

Reality for a large number of mothers is low pay and missing the baby. Although women have flooded into the workplace, joining those working-class women who had never left it, the truth can be grim. They do not all have exciting, rewarding careers and professions. As shown in a survey in *Good Housekeeping* magazine, most mothers do low-paid, part-time work with few rights.

Low pay for mums

If mother knows best, she knows that the truth is that she gets paid the least – less, even, than other woman who do not have children. We know that for too long men have been paid better than women, but research on pay differentials and parenthood by Heather Joshi and Marie Louise Newell showed that childless women earned around 30 per cent more than mothers. Not surprisingly, fathering children did not have the same result. Married men were 10 per cent better off than bachelors on average, but there was little difference between the earnings of fathers and those married men who were childless.

Among Britain's part-time workers, women are heavily represented, making up 90 per cent of the workforce. Of this number, a large proportion are mothers who work 'around family commitments'. Again, in this sector, there is a discrepancy between what men and women earn. According to a report, *Women and Men in Britain*, published by the Equal Opportunities Commission, part-time female manual workers earn only 49 per cent of the basic hourly pay of men doing the same work.

The job trap: settling for less

'Women are certainly capable of learning, but they are not made for the higher forms of science, such as philosophy and certain types of artistic creativity; these require a universal ingredient. Women may hit on good ideas and they may, of course, have taste and elegance, but they lack the talent for the ideal.'

Georg Hegel, 1770–1831, in *The Philosophy of Right*

When shown the results of the *Good Housekeeping* survey, Angela

Rumbold, then Education Minister and member of a ministerial group on women's issues, said, 'I think it's sad that women take so many low-paid jobs – they underrate themselves.'

What was much closer to the truth was that the mothers who answered had taken work which was available near home and had the right hours to enable them to be home after school. This was described by several as a trap. They said mothers 'settled for what they could get', and employers, knowing this, took advantage by offering them jobs with few rights, low pay and little prospect of advancement.

Kirsten described her job as an export clerk: 'Wages here are atrociously low – £3 per hour is considered reasonable for a good secretary in Wiltshire. My husband is in a profession with a very irregular wage. We cannot manage without my pay. The other aspect of the trap with part-time work is that whilst being able to meet my children after school in my 25-hour week, I work an awful lot harder than the full-time employees, and find that I'm often being pressurised into taking on more hours when there is a lot of work to do. Since I cannot take on more hours, I have to work a very concentrated five-hour stretch and arrive home shattered. I feel caught in the trap of having a part-time job conveniently near my home with a regular income.'

Gillian Breen, a local government food technologist, described the effects of the job trap: 'Our materialistic age makes it impossible for one wage to adequately support a young family, so most women will accept low-paid work in the vain hope that it will improve their lifestyle. What it mostly does is exhaust the mother and make the children feel neglected.'

The cost of working

Many working women often cannot afford help and a high proportion of them rely on relatives or partners to care for children, or see a large proportion of their pay go in childcare. Some may consider the children old enough to look after themselves. 'Latchkey children' do not show up in statistics, but the National Out of School Alliance estimates it is something like one in five.

The use of nannies by better-paid and more successful women, although widespread, can take up a great deal of a woman's earnings. Indeed, such women told me that they worked because they loved it and were absorbed, ambitious and involved, but that financially, after paying for childcare, they were not much better off than if they did not work. The growth of nanny-share schemes helps spread the cost.

Sadly, not all women found such fulfilment in their work. There are thousands of women simply struggling with their day on low pay, and feeling that they are missing out on their child's early months or years.

The need for women workers

As the shortage of school leavers bites in the next few years, 900,000 jobs are expected to be taken by women. In 1990, women accounted for one in three of the workforce. By the year 2000, however, according to the Henley Centre for Forecasting, there will be more female employees than male, since three-quarters of all new jobs created in the Nineties will be filled by women. Henley also projects that single-parent families will have increased at five times the rate of dual-parent households during the period from 1989 to 1995. This means that we will be looking at a new shaping of family and work life.

If these new jobs to be filled by women are the sort traditionally filled by first jobbers, pay and prospects will, in all likelihood, be modest. Many of these women returners will have had several years' working experience before taking a break to raise a family (which will have developed further their organisational and managerial skills). Should we then consider it insulting that the Department of Employment and employers expect women to return to work at the very bottom of the ladder, and to step into missing school leavers' shoes?

Some would disagree and are hopeful about women's prospects. There is a view that the demographic time bomb will be good for older, more experienced workers, and that they will find themselves needed and valued. 'Women with qualifications and experience will be very employable. They will quickly make their mark, they are more reliable, have more nous. I think there is real hope that that experience will be tapped,' says editor Polly Toynbee.

The glass ceiling

'Suffer women once to arrive at equality with men, and they will from that moment become our superiors.'

Cato the Elder, 234–149 BC

Another myth about equality and prospects is exploded when

talking to women in differing walks of life. We tend to imagine that the battles are won: women *have* made it into the male world of work and indeed there *are* successful women blazing a trail in all careers. When you look closer, however, you find the question of whether or not the woman is a mother can make all the difference to her success at work.

We need more women with families to humanise the top rungs. The Commission, 'Women at the Top', chaired by Lady Howe, has revealed that 'For too many women there is a glass ceiling over their aspirations – it allows them to see where they might go, but stops them getting there.'

Take, for example, the police force. We are accustomed now to seeing women on the beat, or delicately questioning rape victims or comforting mothers of lost children. But the truth, as the Commission found, is that there are no women above the rank of inspector. In the Civil Service, one in 20 officers in the top seven senior administrative grades is a woman, while in the top three grades women make up only 2 per cent.

> 'The legal system is based on a public school notion of life: silly rules and silly games. The story always goes that clients didn't want women to plead for them because they didn't think they were good enough or that they had authority. The clerk would divide up the work and if he thought, "Well I can't sell you to a solicitor's firm" – then you were lost.'
>
> Lisa Forrell, barrister and theatre director,
> *The Guardian* (7.11.91)

Law attracts women students and they do extremely well academically. But at the time of writing, the Law Lords, the highest court of appeal, has no women members. Of the 27 Appeal Court judges, only one is a woman, while in the High Court the figure drops to one in 87. Out of 434 circuit judges, 17 are women while only 37 of the 1150 QCs are female. One fifth of barristers are female. Although more women qualify as solicitors than men, they are three times more likely to leave the profession in 10 years.

The Law Society has tried to address this problem. They have published *Equal in the Law* and *Equal Opportunities in Solicitors' Firms*, highlighting problems and giving advice. But only four out of the 72 members of its own council are women.

In Parliament, women are dramatically absent – witness the acres of suits visible on television when the debates are broadcast. There are only 44 women out of a total of 650 MPs in the House

of Commons and the House of Lords boasts a mere 73 out of
1184. Apart from the difficulties of selection, one of the major
problems must be the hours. The house sits in the afternoon and
into the night, making the sustaining of a family life difficult for
either sex. The 300 Group, however, is working actively for equal
representation of women in Parliament.

Harriet Harman addressed the House of Commons at 1.37 am
on 9 July 1991 on the subject of the late hours kept by the House:
'This practice is self-imposed or imposed by tradition. If we have
the will and the sense we can change it. How can we [Members
of Parliament] seriously debate on employment, flexible hours,
women returners and childcare when the House cannot change
itself to hear the voices of women?'

At the time of writing there are no women cabinet members in
John Major's government.

Norway has a high percentage of women in government at over
40 per cent, with Sweden a close second with over 30 per cent,
Germany boasts over 10 per cent and France has a poor 5 per cent.

> 'Concerning the fitness of women for politics, there can be no
> question: but the dispute is more likely to turn upon the fitness
> of politics for women.'
>
> Harriet Taylor, partner of John Stewart Mill (1831)

Despite being good organisers and administrators, woman do not
fare well in management posts either. One in nine general managers
and one in four specialist executives are female; two-thirds of
them have middle-ranking status. Fewer than one in a hundred
chief executives are women. Research has shown that 51 per
cent of female managerial staff feel discriminated against in the
workplace.

In a 1990 *Guardian* survey, 58 per cent of the women respondents
believed that levels of sexual discrimination in the workplace
had not changed in 21 years. Joanna Foster, Chair of the Equal
Opportunities Commission, backed this view when she was quoted
in the *Sunday Correspondent* as saying, 'It's the old story of whether
women will get the opportunities to go higher and whether men
will continue to engage in clone recruiting of people like themselves.'

But it is not just a matter of opportunity, but of a radical change
in approach to working mothers. Very few of today's high-flying
career women have the additional responsibility of children: women
are still faced with a stark choice that no man has to make.

Writing in *Balancing Acts: On Being a Mother*, Helena Kennedy, QC, says, 'Motherhood is like some skeleton kept in the cupboard and most of us collaborate in keeping our children invisible. We have the terrible fear that to concede that there are emotional pulls or practical complications will be used against us. In the legal profession it is certainly more acceptable for a male counsel to explain his late arrival because of a car breakdown than it is for a woman counsel to invoke the illness of her child's nanny.'

Leaving the children

As well as problems with pay and prospects, there are emotional difficulties to face, too, when a mother decides to work. In a survey in *Under 5* magazine, 27 per cent of respondents said they would give up work tomorrow if they could. It is hard to generalise, but mothers of under-fives frequently say they would like to be more available to their children. There is a sense of loss and regret at missing out on their children's early years, which amounts to more than simply not being there when the tooth falls out and the chicken pox pop. Other women confirmed this – 'They seem not to miss me too much, but I miss them dreadfully,' wrote Jane Elliot. 'It's all guilt and loss,' said Bea. 'Looking back on it after a year, I must have been potty to go back so early. Life was hell and I was getting by on three or four hours' sleep a night. I missed out on some crucial early months,' said Annette.

Denial of basic instincts

'Women will have achieved true equality not when they are all able to return to full-time work a few weeks after their children are born, but when their role as mothers is given the status it deserves and they are able to plan out their careers on their own terms,' writes teacher Pamela Ormerod. Mothers find they are being forced to go back to work for financial reasons, or because of peer group pressure, very often before they are ready to leave their babies, denying some very basic instincts.

Complying with the regulations on maternity leave is another reason many go back before they feel ready. (In contrast to Britain's minimal provision, maternity leave in Sweden is six or seven months at 90 per cent pay, in Norway 38 weeks on 80 per cent pay). 'You underestimate the close feeling you will have for the baby. I couldn't have imagined I'd feel so torn,' said Lisa as her maternity leave drew to an end.

Hazel Todhunter, a La Leche League breast-feeding counsellor, writes that she often hears from mothers 'who have committed themselves to returning to work before the baby is born, accept maternity pay and then have regrets about having to leave the baby. It is impossible to know in advance the strength of feelings for the young baby or the mother's need to be with the baby – a strong emotional bond. I feel it is the interrupting of this early bond which makes so many working mothers feel guilty. We need much longer statutory maternity leave.'

In *New Mothers at Work*, Julia Brannen and Peter Moss showed the times at which women made their decisions to go back to work. In this study, 61 per cent of the women said that they made their decision to go back before pregnancy, 18 per cent made it during pregnancy, and 14 per cent made it in the first three months following the birth; only 8 per cent made the decision in the second three months when they had got to know their babies.

A crucial phase

Dilys Daws of The Child Psychotherapy Trust describes the minute steps of mutual recognition and adjustment which enable mother and child to become attuned to one another – so necessary in the first weeks. 'I suggest that going through these stages is as crucial psychologically for the mother as for the baby. She is not simply enabling something to happen for the baby, she is also going through an integrating process in her own right . . . finishing a cycle that starts with conception.'

Daws also outlines a problem often mentioned by women expecting to go back to work soon after the birth. The prospect of going back, with the knowledge that there is a future separation looming, breaks into the experience of the early weeks. Paediatrician T. Berry Brazelton has described how this looming separation interferes with the bonding process, when parents defend themselves against too intense an attachment because of the imminent pain of separating prematurely from the baby. He implies that the impending separation robs parents of intimacy ahead of time. Mothers, for example, concentrate on getting the child into a suitable schedule – suitable for their work requirements that is – forcing timetables upon a period which should be timeless. 'It seems as though the experience of the early weeks of babyhood needs to be timeless and thus infinite to be fully enjoyed by mother and baby,' writes Daws. She argues that mothers who go back to work too early are missing out on the vital freedom to 'follow a natural timetable for you and the baby – that slow dreamy time which helps the baby establish his own physiological and emotional rhythm.'

Pat Garrett's experience illustrates the dilemma. She describes her anguish when her breastfed baby refused to switch to a bottle when she was due to go back to work. She was told that someone else should offer the bottle, so 'I spent a whole day outside that lounge door listening to these screams and rows as this baby refused to be fed. I thought, what am I doing to this child, what a selfish mother I am to let this child suffer.'

Who needs mothers anyway?

'I grew up in the Fifties and Sixties, so in my twenties and thirties I thought staying home and having kids was distinctly uncool.' This view of mothering has been pervasive during the last two decades. Women also point out that their surge into the workplace and the rise of the women's movement have combined to have a negative impact on the way mothers are viewed. Mothers feel they are undervalued whether or not they work outside the home.

On becoming a mother, a woman may feel she has ceased to be part of society in a variety of ways, both major and minor. She becomes that invisible person pushing a pram, not an attractive girl walking down the street. 'Once you're behind a pram you're neutralised,' says Eveline. You're said to be wasting your education and training, vegetating, doing nothing. This can cause loss of confidence and effect a woman's search for work when she does go back, preparing her in a way to settle for whatever she can get.

Mothers complain of being devalued, and protest that they are not catered for in public transport, town planning, store design and public amenities. 'I was surrounded by a world that cooed and gurgled at my baby but was hostile to me. Getting around with a pram was a battle on poorly designed kerbs, steps and public transport. Shopping became a nightmare. Being expected to feed my baby in a toilet made me realise that mothers and toddlers were not considered in any aspect of public life,' explains Irene, an accountant.

Sally, a full-time mother for a few years, grew tired of being asked at dinner parties, 'What do you do?' with its implication that without paid work one did nothing. So she developed a reply: 'I grow girls,' reasoning that if she had replied that she bred horses the answer would be, 'How interesting!'

Macho mothering

Some women, particularly career-oriented women in certain fields, are pressured to collude in creating a negative view of mothers – as though resisting the involvement and pull of motherhood is to be admired. There is a defiance, almost a braggadocio, like saying to motherhood, 'I dare you to change my life.' This can cause peer group pressure on other women who feel obliged to do the same because it has become the norm in the office for women to take off only a couple of weeks after giving birth, and to carry on as though they have been on a trip to the Bahamas instead of the labour ward.

Writing of this phenomenon in her book *Balancing Acts: On Being a Mother*, Helena Kennedy, a QC and mother of two, coined the phrase 'macho mothering'. She used it to describe how women in the legal profession vied with each other about how little time they took off to have babies, and how they bragged about nannies and night feeds and about shunting their children off to boarding school. 'Women with children, I realised, compartmentalise their domestic and public lives,' Helena continued. 'The unspoken rule is never to mix the two, or involve one in aid of the other. The image of the capable woman must never be tainted by the smell of baby powder.'

Private life

'A wife made to order can't compare with a ready maid.'

Joke

Being both a mother and a worker also involves a degree of personal loss. Women have believed for some time that to go all out for a career is to sacrifice one's private life. Jane Lapotaire, actress and mother, is aware of this: 'Women still think being success-ful professionally will mean your private life suffers, which of course it does. Work, children have priority – there are only 24 hours a day – the men get what's left over. But they've been

giving us those kind of leftovers for years . . . I think male
sexuality is linked with ego and women's sexuality isn't. That
is, if he's successful, he's sexually attractive. If she's successful
she's a ball-breaker. I think the sexual side of women's ego is
bound up with her biology, which has a nurturing function.'
(From an interview in *Inspirational Women* by Nikki Henriques.)

A new way

Perhaps the answer is for women not merely to join the male-
dominated system but to imbue it with new values. 'Macho management has failed,' claims Dr Beverly Alimo-Metcalfe; and now
women should demonstrate the value of female attributes. She
claims that widely used selection techniques and assessment procedures contain 'hidden barriers' for women. They take men as
their models: this requires applicants to adopt the style of those
already in the job.

Women were just as capable but were perceived by their assessors
as less efficient because their methods differed. Women succeeded
by motivating staff, by being visionaries and catalysts, generating
ideas and attracting colleagues and subordinates towards the aims
of the organisation. 'The military method of management (relying
on punishment and reward) has had its day,' she says.

Jean Baker Miller, in her book *Towards a New Psychology of Women*,
describes women's experiences as 'being on the cutting edge of a
new and larger vision . . . For this vision to flourish, women will
have to create new social institutions to support and enlarge it . . .
the real motivation for a new form of living today arises in women
out of intensely felt personal needs.'

In the future, rather than mimic men's style, we will have to
try and mould the patriarchal society around our feminine curves.
Instead of a race to the finish in which women stumble over
domestic and emotional obstacles, we need to navigate a route
for both sexes around all the problems, helping each other over
the hurdles.

Real-life stories

To illustrate what it is really like to be a working mother, let us take a look at the experiences of some real people. Dorothy Chapman and her husband were both medical students. They decided to marry at the end of their residence year (a period of working 100 hours a week). Then their careers began to diverge. Dorothy writes, 'My choice of career in medicine was very much influenced by his as I did not wish to compete with him for jobs and did not want to work at the other end of the country.'

She trained as a GP but found that when she went for interviews the talk always got round to, 'What does your husband do?' and 'I see you have no children, what are your plans?' Because of this, Dorothy gave up trying to get a job as GP principal, and took work in the Civil Service, locums, and as a clinical assistant.

Because of a system which is highly competitive, offering short-term contracts and moving people about the country until they get their final job, married women are at an extreme disadvantage. You cannot say, "I wish to be a specialist in . . . and live in . . .",' writes Dorothy. 'You just apply for and take the best jobs you can get wherever they are. This is extremely stressful and that, added to the hours you work, can make life very hard.' For all these reasons, she decided that her husband's career had to take priority if she was to stay happily married. She loves her work, however, and says that without her family attachments it could take over her life completely.

Many of Dorothy's friends have decided not to have children 'as it will interfere with their career prospects'. This seems a pity because those women doctors who do have a family life have so much to offer their patients in terms of understanding and experience of life – and of course, first-hand knowledge of children.

Dorothy's case is no exception: her experience is common. Isobel Allen has done a survey aimed at finding out why many women fail to achieve their full potential in medicine. The study found that nearly 50 per cent of women who qualified in 1966 and 1976 are now working part-time in non-training posts, in what many describe as dead-end jobs. Allen concluded that the rigid and conventional medical career structure makes no allowances for women to have children and that many more part-time career opportunities should be made available. Almost half the medical students we now train are women. In 1988–9, 45.6 per cent of medical students were women.

Although we are at the end of the twentieth century, in some ways little seems to have changed. According to a report by Saffron Davies, published in September 1987 in the *Guardian*, the percentages of women in different sectors of the medical profession were as follows:

21% of GPs
13.8% of consultants
0.6% of general surgery consultants
4.6% of general medicine consultants
12% of obstetrics and gynaecology consultants
22% of paediatrics consultants
38% of child and adolescent consultants

The glass ceiling – through which women can glimpse where they want to go but cannot reach – is in place.

During World War I, doctors had been urgently needed. In 1914 there was an appeal from the leaders of the medical profession for women to train to replace men. Many teaching hospitals opened their doors to women. At the end of the war, when surviving men doctors returned, these hospitals generally went back to refusing women. The senior physician at Westminster tried to soften the blow by assuring girls that there was absolutely nothing against them except their sex. Their devoted service during the war was appreciated, but was only needed during the time of national emergency. The view were that 100 per cent of male trainee would stay in the profession while 50 per cent of women would leave to marry.

We may laugh at these remarks, but the truth is that women are still facing this agonising choice in medicine. Unless the profession restructures itself to enable women to have a family life and remain active in their chosen profession and in the mainstream for promotion, the loss to the country will be enormous. Why should women still be facing this choice of family life or career when most families would prefer doctors with a mother's experience?

Women make up only 12 per cent of the country's obstetricians – gynaecologists. Mrs Susan Blunt, a consultant, describes the problem: 'The career is very challenging and stimulating. You can deliver a baby one day and be dealing with a granny's prolapse the next. I really love it. But the structure is a nightmare and a real turn-off. It just affects women so much more than men. The training is twice as long as most other specialities. By the time you are ready to become a senior registrar you are in your thirties and you are lucky if you are a consultant by the time you are 40. If you take a few years out to have a family, you will never become a consultant; but if you wait until you have become one it may be too late. There you are lecturing to people about having babies and you can't have one yourself.' (*The Times* 7.11.1991.)

Doctors are not the only women to face this dilemma. Rhuna is a highly regarded cello teacher, teaching at famous music schools and privately. 'It wasn't so much that I couldn't have gone on, because lots of people do. It was having to make that choice,' she told me. 'I played at the English National Opera, I thought of myself as a musician and you suddenly realised it wasn't like that at all. If you did that then you didn't see much of your children. Really, what took me by surprise was the depth of feeling for the children, because, before Vanora was born, I can honestly say that I had in my mind that I was a musician, and I just didn't see how I could be a musician in the way that I wanted. I thought it was a terribly hard choice and I don't know if I'd make the same one.'

Rhuna's daughters are now working at careers in their turn and she notices among their friends that they're 'not all that keen on having children', a consequence perhaps of becoming committed to a career.

Rhuna added thoughtfully, 'It's a very hard thing to go through, that, you don't see a way out. I didn't want to become some sort of housekeeper/nanny. All the same I didn't want to miss out on all the terribly exciting and rewarding time with the children.' She compared her field of work to others and concluded that 'in a way musicians at least have a choice. I had a choice in that I knew that I could do teaching, although I didn't actually want to at all then, I was not the slightest bit interested in teaching. I wanted to play.

But lots of people in business don't have that choice, so in a way, they've got to have a nanny.'

In many cases, women restructured their careers to fit in with their families. They did not stop working, but took on fewer hours, less responsibility and less chance of promotion.

Expectation and reality

There is a widening gap between expectation and reality. Girls are encouraged through education and talk of equality to assume they will go into the career of their choice if they're good enough. There is little or no preparation for parenthood and, with no support structure, new mothers are forced to make individual compromises and personal arrangements for their children.

Facing up to the possibility that you will have to rethink your work life comes as a cruel shock when a mother realises how short maternity leave is, how little childcare is around, how expensive it is, and how difficult it is to leave the baby.

Women seldom take these difficulties into account when choosing a career. When I spoke to university students about their career hopes, very few had even thought about what life with children might mean. They were so busy competing on equal terms at university and in the job stakes that they had no time to look up from their studies and think about the long term.

Younger women expect a career and see childbirth as a slight blip in the graph. The shock of deep attachment to the child, and the new permanent responsibility takes some getting used to.

Cindy Chant, a health visitor giving parentcraft classes, finds a universal ignorance about parenting. She teaches throughout the year and finds her 'student mothers' quite unprepared. She thinks this contributes to the amount of postnatal depression she is seeing. 'I think the postnatal scars are high and getting higher as mothers today are not prepared for the reality. They do not grow up in large families. They do not learn parentcraft/mothering skills, the extended family is fading, their common sense is poor, most of them come from split families anyway. The emphasis seems to be on a career structure to provide a good salary.' Much of what I heard confirmed this: 'Motherhood is a real shock. I had no idea', 'I feel sick with the responsibility', 'Nothing prepared me for this'.

There is also the place mothering has in society. Adjusting to this high ideal yet low status is not easy. In her chapter in *Balancing*

Acts, entitled 'The World Is a More Dangerous Place', Victoria Hardie writes: 'For the first time I was thrown into a world that did not recognise my physical, emotional, social and political needs. This applied to design, architecture, roads, public transport, dangerous machinery, not to mention lack of community childcare facilities.'

Missing person

Reality can mean realising that the comforting 'make-it-better' mother figure is missing in your family's life. The way in which careers are structured seems to be based on the assumption in the workplace that each striving career person is supported by a 'wife' figure at home. This supportive nurturer, it is believed, will take all homecare responsibilities off the shoulders of the career person, and provide emotional support too. When the wife is herself striving careerwise, the family can unconsciously feel the lack of this 'mothering' and almost wish that a warm motherly figure would magically appear in their midst to make it all better, to take care of them, to comfort and support them, listen for hours to their problems, cook their favourite foods, iron that special shirt in time for the meeting and send them off each morning with a smile.

In her absence, both partners carry the strain of doing the third career – homemaking in addition to their jobs. Couples talk of an awareness that this figure is missing in their lives, and speak of a 'gaping hole', and a wish for a mother figure. As one busy solicitor and mother put it: 'I need a wife.'

'Where is the butter?'

It seems that when this 'gaping hole' is felt by the children and spouse they react in various ways to reclaim mum's attention. One of these is the 'Where is the butter?' syndrome. Carol coined this phrase to describe those requests which are transparent calls for attention – for the object being sought is always in the same and obvious place. The butter is always in the fridge or on the table – where else? Simply asking for it perpetuates the 'helpless' pose of a child or spouse. It is laying claim once more to that 'make-it-better' mum who provides everything for everyone, and an attempt to push real-life mothers into this fantasy rôle.

A working mother will often make a brave attempt to train her family out of this habit, but many report that when there are members feeling the lack of her emotional nurturing presence they revert to this pattern. 'Where is the butter?' joins 'Have you seen my glasses?' or even 'Where are my car keys?' This can deteriorate to 'Where have *you put* my car keys?' making mum the omnipotent doer of everything even when she is absent all day!

This tendency can be very draining and can severely add to the early morning rush. Some women feel that it may be a sign of underlying anxiety, while others dismiss it as simply laziness. There are those who recommend a little extra love and attention at other more convenient times to make a child feel secure, while others simply retort, 'Get it yourself.'

Adapting to change

Life demands that women are adaptable. They must be able to cope with several major life changes. Penny, for example, has had periods of vastly different work experience, been married twice, been a single parent for a while, and has recently been a mature student. Her story is not unusual and shows how women need to prepare for a life with several twists and turns.

Penny started working when her first husband left her with two children. Prior to this, she had been a full-time mother. She began as a secretary at the BBC and worked her way up to become a production administrator, responsible for the allocation of studios, crews and resources. During this time she felt she had to make a new life and provide for her children.

The job grew and Penny was holding a great deal of responsibility. When she remarried, she found herself integrating two more children into the family. 'It was an amalgamation of two families really, requiring adjustments all round,' she says. At this time, her job was demanding and involved extensive travel. She deputised for her boss for six months, and later was offered a promotion which meant even more travel. 'The children were 11, 12, 14 and 15. That's when I realised I just wasn't giving them enough time. I thought, well, I really can't handle this, I would have been away two weeks at a time. Having turned that down, I really started to think.'

Penny weighed things up: 'Obviously I could have taken it but I would have suffered.' When the children were younger, she had always felt that she missed out more than they did. They came home from school, were well cared for and provided for until she got in from work, but she missed all their eager chatter after school. Now with teenagers on the scene and four children instead of two, the decisions were different and less clear-cut: 'There was some sort of CND march and both the girls wanted to go and we had to sit down and discuss the pros and cons, and I suddenly thought there are going to be more of these sorts of things – helping them make decisions . . .'

Penny decided to leave her stressful job and opened her own business, a toy shop very near home. Now she was available if a child needed to ask her something and, although she worked long hours, she could break off for family suppers and go back to finish later. She could organise a deputy to free her for a school event, or a doctor's appointment: work was more in her own control. 'That was becoming a problem at the BBC. Obviously the higher up the ladder, the less easy it is. There is an important meeting which clashes with Speech Day – what do you do?'

This worked well for all: 'I've talked to my children quite a lot about it. I think they're being honest when they say they were very glad that I worked. They said, "Thank God you can talk about interesting things." '

Penny talked of responsibility and decision making. 'Although the shop work meant long hours and a responsibility,' she says, 'it wasn't as pressured as my job at the BBC so I was less tired, more able to cope with teenage discussion.' The difference in the shop job was that events were directly under her control: 'Being my own boss as opposed to problems you can't control in a big organisation, and you may not get on with your boss.'

Penny's own mother had been a buyer in a department store, and she feels it is helpful to have seen your own mother work. Both of her daughters have gone into professions, one a doctor and one a teacher. Penny is pleased about this: 'I think it's much more important for girls to have a proper training and a profession they can go back to or continue with if they don't marry or whatever. It's so much easier for the boys to get jobs.'

Now Penny has completed a degree as a mature student. She has enjoyed this and was able to give more time to her family. She is rethinking yet again: 'It's a very nice, stimulating sort of world, university, and I was accepted very much as a student. Now it would be nice to give something back. I might teach.'

Penny's story makes up a patchwork of working and parenting entwined into a satisfying whole. It is no mean feat to have integrated two families successfully, or to have brought up four children, or held down any one of her jobs. Now there is her degree. Perhaps we should break away from the linear, ladder-like structure of careers and see that there is strength in variety, in being adaptable.

Taking the initiative

'We have no desire to say anything that might tend to encourage women to embark on accountancy, for although women might make excellent book-keepers there is much in accountancy proper that is, we think, unsuitable for them.'
    Accountant, English Institute of Chartered Accountants, 1912

Finding that it is a man's world out there has caused many women to take charge of their lives. They solve many of the work/family dilemmas by setting up on their own as Penny did, or taking on a franchise. Being your own boss appeals. Women lead the franchise field: out of the 125,000 British franchises existing in 1990, 83,000 were run by women.

Men have always had networks operating on the basis of mutual self-interest, and now women are learning how important and useful these are. Women Into Business has set up a directory of contacts available to fellow members, while the Medical Women's Federation monitors conditions in the profession for women. The City Women's Network and Women In Publishing are just two of the other, similar organisations women have set up.

A question of guilt

Despite the ever-rising numbers of mothers out at work (in the USA, 68 per cent of women with children under 18 are in the workforce, and 60 per cent in the UK), these women, more than any other generation it seems, are plagued with guilt and conflict over their dual roles. One after the other, women tell of guilt nagging away in the background.

'I feel guilty because . . .

'. . . I can't be the kind of mother I want to be'

'. . . I feel I should be with the children more'

'. . . my home responsibilities make inroads on my effectiveness at work'

'. . . there is no time for my partner and me to share'

'. . . I can't be there for the children as my mother was'

'. . . I'm so tired, I have no patience'

'. . . I'm not there when they need me'

Today's working mother has none of the certainty of a wartime Rosie the Riveter, doing her bit for the country. When she was growing up she probably knew many children whose mothers were at home at least during the early years of their lives.

Rôle models of successful working mothers are only now becoming apparent. At the top of the career ladder, there is still an elite band of successful women who have remained childless, who have found it impossible to combine the two. They are testimony to the difficulties of the dual rôle choice.

Women constantly question whether they have made the right decision. Even those women who seem to have it all – successful career and a loving family with four children – admit that the guilt is always there somewhere, waiting to pounce. 'I talk about it all the time, I think about it, talk to the other women at work – perhaps we should give it all up and buy a house in the country and write a book and live a quieter life and look after the children,' says Polly Toynbee, Social Affairs Editor at the BBC. 'We all go through this at least once a day; it's the universal fantasy where you give it all up. I've always had that and I don't suppose I shall ever do it, and if I did I think I'd go mad.'

Working mothers tell of their emotions swirling around in a soup of guilt in which many different ingredients contribute flavour and piquancy. There are times when one ingredient dominates all others, or moments where two or three combine to overwhelm the taste, but women are learning to keep the flavours in balance.

Mother knows best

So how are we to deal with these feelings of guilt and anxiety that undeniably exist today? To understand how this pervasive feeling of guilt arose, and perhaps to come to terms with it, we need to stand back from our own personal experience and see how it is set in an historical context.

Certainly, one of the key ingredients in the 'soup of guilt' is the influence our mothers had on us. A daughter's relationship with her mother can be very intense, affecting her outlook in ways of which she is barely aware.

Simone de Beauvoir recognised this invisible bond when she wrote of the profound effect her mother had on her: 'And this is how we lived, the two of us, in a kind of symbiosis. Without striving to imitate her, I was conditioned by her.'

In many subtle – and not so subtle – ways, our mothers have passed on to us their ideas on mothering, ideas rooted in a time very different from our own. As Sylvia Ann Hewlitt asks in her book *A Lesser Life*: 'But why were all of us so passionately vested in being all-providing, all-encompassing mothers to our children? And why did we take direct responsibility for moulding perfect human beings despite being liberated modern women?' She goes on to show that the explanation lies in our heritage, for 'not only do we carry the normal load of mothers – we love our children unreasonably and irrationally – but, in addition, we have inherited (many of us unknowingly) the most powerful cult of motherhood this world has ever seen.' (The cult of motherhood is discussed in greater detail in Part One.)

A woman's place

A generation of post-war babies, brought up in the old traditional way by at-home mothers, has now switched to working motherhood. For many life did not turn out to be a matter of simply finding Mr Right but a juggling act with working life and family demands when we had not even planned to join the circus. 'I grew up in a culture where a girl was successful if she made a good marriage . . . nobody ever showed me the value of a career for oneself,' says accounts assistant Geraldine Hughes.

There is now a revolution going on as women who carry within them the conditioning and influence of their mothers try to forge new patterns of living. Eve, actress and mother of two, expressed this when we talked about her mother's expectations for her. She felt she had been 'conditioned' and had been unable to go 'the whole way towards a full-time career'. She found a solution, working part-time in radio and doing voice work which enabled her to be with her children a great deal.

'Well, I always thought of myself as an actress, but I was very conditioned by my mother, terribly conditioned and although I saw myself as an actress she saw me as a potential mother – that was the rôle for any woman in life. I think that was one of the reasons I didn't pursue my career. I was always slightly scared, I always felt underneath that if I pursued my career I wouldn't fulfil what was expected of me by my mother.'

Like thousands of others, Eve describes feeling 'slightly scared' to deviate from the rôle cut out for her. There were fewer rôle models of successful working mothers around then, these women were trailblazing. Is it any wonder they have moments of doubt?

Keeping up standards

Again and again, women describe a compulsion to do things as well as their mothers or other women. Modern woman still has a legacy of the mothering she received. On the one hand feminism devalued mothering and homemaking until a woman felt embarrassed to admit she was 'just a housewife'. On the other Superwoman seemed to be good at everything.

Women feel a duty and a drive to do right by their families. When they cannot live up to these unspoken demands they feel guilty at 'failing', when the truth is it is impossible to keep up that style of living in a non-traditional lifestyle.

Dorothy, a busy doctor, describes the dilemma. Although she has some help and has her life well organised, she still measures herself against the only mothering she knew. After speaking of the way in which her husband, also a doctor, does his share so well, Dorothy still feels, 'Despite all this support, I still get intense guilt feelings about working because my own mum didn't.'

This is the voice of a generation in transition, looking forward to a new life of working and parenting, while also looking back to how it used to be when they were children. Of course distance clouds the memory and time lends a rosy hue so that far-off childhood seems either more ideal than it actually was, or more agonising, and we resolve to do things differently.

Looking over our shoulders at the 'perfect' homes our mothers kept, we go forward into a future where we cannot possibly lead a non-traditional life while clinging to traditional values. But the experience of our formative years dies hard. There is a gut feeling – and social reinforcement – that we should be there when our children come home from school, should have a hot meal on the table when our husbands come in, should be wife, mother, guardian of health, educator, protector of the family's moral values, hostess, decorator, gardener, partner and lover – to say nothing of doing all the maintenance tasks such as the laundry and shopping and keeping a spotless home. It is an anachronistic idea that the mother should be the sole guardian and keeper of the home, servicing the needs of all family members even while she holds down a job.

In *Balancing Acts*, Helena Kennedy describes her own attempts to measure up to her mother's standards. 'Mothering was big business in our home,' she says. 'My mother still feels good about herself as a producer of babies and carer of children . . . I still fantasise about being the perfect mother. I save old bones at the back of the fridge in the vague hope of making stock and cock-a-leekie soup like my mother's. I hoard egg cartons and bottle tops for inspired artwork with my offspring. I bake birthday cakes in the shape of Thomas the Tank Engine; all we need is a bit of soft focus on the lens and I am as good as any of those mothers in the TV ads.'

Some women find themselves going to extraordinary lengths to match up to these invisible inner criteria. 'It's part of the guilt thing you have as a working mother in a sense,' says Penny. 'I really had to work, but nevertheless I found I set myself far too high standards. I mean the birthday cake had to be as good as or, if possible, better than the other child's birthday cake whose mother had had all day to ice it. I'd be up till two in the morning the night before the birthday party.' (Penny was by this time working at a very senior level in television administration, and had a gruelling day ahead.)

With our own experience of mothering so different from that of our mothers, we find ourselves standing astride a crevasse of guilt with one foot firmly in the kitchen and the other foot commuting to work. One slip and we're caught by the nagging doubts. Am I doing the right thing? Will this harm the children? Should I have done things differently? Am I letting my boss down? How can I satisfy my family and my work demands? Is it a game we cannot win? Kirsten described the struggle and the backsliding so aptly: 'Parenting and working is like a game of Snakes and Ladders,' she said.

If we are not to continue under this burden of guilt and exhaustion, we need to look more closely at our unexamined assumptions about the way things *should* be. 'What is changing today, is the correlation between the ideal and the norm,' says Patricia Hewitt, co-author of *The Family Way*, a paper by the Institute for Public Policy Research, 'between how people think family life ought to be lived and how people are actually living. What used to be a fairly strong correlation is becoming weaker.' The result is a sense of dissatisfaction, a feeling that somehow families are missing out on family life as they imagine it to be – and that somehow this is the mother's fault.

A happy compromise

If guilt at falling short of your mother's standards is a common reaction, rebellion is another. 'It is important, also, to realise,' writes Anne Oakley in *Subject Women*, 'that a daughter who consciously rejects her mother's influence is defining herself in relation to her.' Juliana shows this clearly: 'My mother's life was humiliating. My sister and I decided not to do the same thing. Men had power. I wanted some of it.'

But it is possible, though, to come to recognise that there is value in both your own and your mother's lifestyles. When a woman is confident of her own ideas for living, and happy in her dual career, it becomes easier to acknowledge the value of her mother's views, without slavishly following them.

Although she admits that even as a young girl she was distancing herself from her mother's ways, Shirley Abott writes lovingly of her in *Mothers* (ed. Susan Cahill): 'I myself have become some sort of urban, educated feminist, and my mother and I are still at cross purposes. Particularly since my daughters were born, she has whispered in my ear each night as I slept, trying to remake me in her image. I battle her off as well as I can, but she touches me still and I love her. I would not want my children to grow up without knowing what their grandmother thought.'

We will have to forge new life patterns and show our children that there is more than one right way to live. Can we avoid setting up a new rigid blueprint – that of superwoman? For if we set her up as the ideal we condemn our children to guilt or rebellion in their turn.

Letting down the boss

'While we all realise you *must* have time off to have a baby, do you *have* to leave, couldn't you just take a longer lunch hour?'
                                                    Words in a greeting card

Even if we manage to come to terms with our mothering, we still face another major worry: are we doing our jobs properly? As women, we may fear that we are taking too much time off work because our children are sick, or that in other ways our being mothers prevents us from being satisfactory workers.

But is any of this guilt and worry well founded? Women in the *Good Housekeeping* survey showed that, in fact, very few days were missed from work on account of their children. Some women wrote that they felt pressure to perform well despite sleepless nights with a child, and even to return to work soon after giving birth for fear of letting the image of women down. 'In both cases I worked full time until the week before they were born and went back within 10–12 weeks. I was very conscious that if people thought my pregnancy interfered with my work other women might suffer,' wrote Dorothy Chapman, a doctor.

The attitudes at work of employers and colleagues are powerful influences, acting in tandem with society's denigration of motherhood. 'It's almost as if there's a caste system of employment, and motherhood is down there at the bottom,' wrote Dabney McKenzie in *Time* magazine.

Women carry the burden of responsibility with them always. If a child is ill, for example, it is seldom the father who will take time off work to stay home. Indeed, society on the one hand decrees that the mother's place is beside her sick child, and sniffs critically at the mother who works, while at the same time the world of work expects her to turn in a faultless performance. 'If I come to work in a bad state after a night up with the baby there is resentment and comment, but if my male colleague comes in with a hangover that's acceptable,' says Bea.

Women report that they try to carry on regardless, fearful lest their jobs be jeopardised and fearful lest all women be judged by the performance of one. There is a sense in which women still feel they need to prove themselves and therefore try very hard to be conscientious and responsible in the workplace. Is it any wonder, then, that they experience conflict and guilt?

What the experts say

There is a deeply held feeling that children of working mothers suffer. *Time* magazine did a survey in December 1989 in which women were asked, 'Which do you think suffers most: marriage, children or career?' They answered 28 per cent, 42 per cent and 12 per cent respectively. These views, however, are not borne out by research.

There have been several professional studies looking at children of working mothers. Their findings are, on the whole, reassuring – if one can generalise and divide women so arbitrarily into two groups without allowing for the finer gradations of how many hours they work and how good the substitute care is. How good a mother each of us is seems unquantifiable.

Sheila B. Kamerman and Cheryl Hayes edited *Children of Working Parents: Experience and Outcomes in 1983*, in which they reviewed previous research on the children of working mothers. They concluded that a mother's employment has no consistent ill effects on a child's school achievement, IQ, or social and emotional development. In fact, studies have shown that children, particularly girls, may benefit from a positive rôle model and that, where working mothers are happy in their dual rôles, they act as a spur to independence and confidence for their children.

Lois Hoffman, social psychologist at the University of Michigan, charted 50 years of research and concluded that most girls of all social classes and boys from working-class families whose mothers worked were more self-confident and earned better grades than children whose mothers were housewives. But she also found that, compared to sons of housewives, middle-class boys raised by working mothers did not do so well and were less confident. It seems this group needed more input from mother, or that middle-class stay-at-home mothers gave greater time and attention to their sons.

Professor Butterworth at Stirling University believes, 'There is no reason to suppose that a child who is well looked after in a crêche and is loved by its parents will suffer any damage. You can see a crêche as an extended family group providing other children to play with.'

But most fascinating of all is the work of Dr Bengt-Erik Andersson, of the Stockholm Institute of Education, who studied 128 children over many years. He found that those who were in day care from the age of one or two performed better at school: 'They had better concentration, were less anxious and were more assertive when it came to standing up for their opinions,' said Dr Andersson. 'The transition from pre-school to school was more smooth and they were more socially confident and articulate.'

Following his research into the effects of day care on children up to the age of eight, Andersson did a follow-up study to age 13. Children were classified according to the type of early childcare they had and their age at first entry into this care. When eight years old, the children who had entered day care before the age of one, but later than six months, were rated more favourably by their teachers than other children.

'They performed better in all school subjects and were regarded as more persistent, independent, more assertive (in a positive sense), less anxious and with better verbal facility. They had an easy transition from pre-school to school and finally they performed better in intellectual tests. At 13 years old, the positive ratings of those children entering day care before the age of one remained. They performed better in all school subjects and were popular, more open and with better verbal facility but also somewhat less quiet than other children.'

Andersson emphasises the difficulty of comparing one study of the effects of day care with another because of the wide variation in types of care offered. He also stresses the importance of the Swedish family support system. This allows parents the right to stay home and look after their newborn infant without the risk of losing their jobs. At the time of the study, this period was six months. It is now 15 months. Because of this mothers who decide to work during their infant's first months do so by choice rather than necessity. During their leave, parents are guaranteed 90 per cent of their previous salary paid by a social insurance system.

Andersson also points to the importance of high-quality day care when parents do return to work. In Sweden, care is of a consistently high standard, provided either in day-care centres or as family day care (childminders). The day-mothers are hired and licensed by the municipalities. They are encouraged to take part in short courses for day-mothers. They are paid even when a child is sick and also get paid vacations. The municipality provides a substitute if the day-mother is ill.

The critical factors in Sweden are the parents' initial months of bonding with the new infant, the availability of parental leave to care for a sick child and the excellent quality of day care on offer. The aim of the centres is not only to provide care but also to provide educational stimulation. By tradition, the stimulation of social and personal development has been considered more important than intellectual development or school preparation. However, the new pre-school programme emphasises cognitive aims as well. In addition, there are open pre-schools for day-mothers and mothers not working outside the home. They can take their children to the pre-school where the children meet and play with others and the parents meet others and can get advice or support in their caring rôle from a trained pre-school teacher.

The Andersson study shows what good results can be obtained from a sound family support system. Working parents can feel relaxed and secure in the knowledge that their children are getting this high-quality care. Families are supported in their parenting, whether or not the mothers work. Children are valued and cherished as the nation recognises their importance for the future.

Compare the Swedish model with the package of arrangements so many British mothers are forced to make, with a combination of people looking after a child. There may be different friends or relatives on different days, with as many as three or four different carers slotting in to make up a jigsaw to cover working hours. Here is the scheme that Jane Elliot, for example, has put together to enable her to work. Her husband works a night shift, so he is at home when the children come from school and nursery. He gives them tea and prepares the adults' meal. 'A friend collects my boys from school and brings them home. (I take hers to school with mine each morning.) Same friend child minds in the holidays. Elderly next-door neighbours collect three-year-old daughter from nursery twice a week. My daughter is at nursery three full days and my mother has her two full days.'

With arrangements such as these, only one person has to let the mother down for the whole house of cards to collapse. The resulting tension and worry on her part makes itself felt, and some children get passed like parcels from one carer to another, hardly knowing with whom they are to be left next. Mothers make up care packages with one carer looking after a child before school and perhaps three or four different ones in the afternoons after nursery school is out. Informal arrangements with friends mean looking after their children on days when mothers are at home, thus limiting still further the time alone with their own children.

We need to build up family support systems and childcare which is available and reasonable, with the costs becoming tax deductible. Then mothers can be free of the guilt about their children, for they will thrive, and the mothers can become reliable workers, benefiting both employers and the economy.

Whatever makes you happy . . .

A mother's emotional wellbeing clearly affects the quality of her mothering. Women said that because they found some fulfilment and sense of self-worth in their work life, they were better mothers, and there is no doubt that an at-home mother who resents her lot is harmful to her children. Most experts state that what affects the child is how the mother herself feels about her rôle, rather than whether or not she works.

Dilys Daws of the Tavistock Clinic points to a survey in her book *Through the Night*, in which mothers of pre-school children with conflicting emotions about being full-time mothers and housewives – feeling a duty to stay at home but feeling dissatisfied with this and wanting to work – were four times as likely to have been prescribed sedatives, tranquillisers and other similar medication in the previous year as those who experienced no such conflict. In the same way, mothers who are dissatisfied with their work lives and do not feel content with their lifestyle, feeling torn and resentful, may be offering less to their children when they are together.

Research shows that better emotional health can be the result of entering the workforce. Extremely busy women may have a sense of wellbeing, a positive self-image and satisfaction with life. In fact, going to work sometimes alleviated emotional stress at home. 'The workplace can sometimes seem like a health spa compared to life at home,' concluded the authors of *Lifeprints*, Grace Baruch, Rosalind Barnett and Carol Rivers.

Polly Toynbee also thinks a working mother can be better for the child's emotional health. There is a sense of claustrophobia in her description of a home with a stay-at-home mother: 'The home is a kind of vacuum which exists in the middle of nowhere with its own rituals and worries. It's much less intense [for me because] I'm not sitting there thinking . . . and she hasn't tidied her room again. It's not something I've been festering about, waiting for her to come home from school.'

Penny agrees: 'The thing about the mother being at home is she has so much time to be always fussing – "Have you got your jersey on?" If you're out at work the child has to take on that responsibility.'

Polly argues that a working mother brings 'a connection with the outside world – particularly with me and my husband because we are so involved with news and events'. She explains that this gives a child a sense of 'what earning money is like, what working relationships are like, what you have to do in order to be an employee, where you fit into the world and how it is a family fits into the world'. She goes on to explain that, even if a job is humble, people get enormous satisfaction out of being employed: it is 'this whole idea that I'm worth something because somebody out there bothers to pay me. I belong. I fit in. I do something and this company needs me and I have a small part to play in it.'

Polly's views echo the words of Winifred Holtby, writing way back in 1934 in her book *Women and a Changing Civilisation*: 'Mothers who can share their children's interests, mothers who have some knowledge of the wider world outside the family circle, are far better equipped than purely domestic housewives to help their sons and daughters . . .'

What the children say

Many children, too, talk proudly of their mother's work and value their contribution to society. One or two commented that the fact that their mothers worked gave them a lot more personal space as the mother's energy was not focused entirely on the child. Clare said she enjoyed having some time to herself after school before her mother got in from work and said she thought they got on better as a result.

It is a strain to be the focus of your mother's attention and in the spotlight all the time, say some of the older children I have spoken to. They explain that they think a child can carry too much of a burden of hopes and fears of their parents, particularly if there are no other siblings and the mother has few outside interests. They wonder, 'Can I really satisfy all those hopes and dreams?' This was seldom brought up by children from large families.

Of course, there are many mothers who do not do paid work but who are creative, busy and fulfilled with other interests. This was discussed but, as the children pointed out, if she was pursuing a hobby she would seldom have to be away when you needed her, so she was in a way always available and they enjoyed this.

As these children grow to adulthood, it is highly likely that they will accept the idea of the working mother as the norm and, in doing so, will walk free of the anxiety and worry that has so marked their mothers. It is also possible that the next generation will grow to maturity with new views on the rôles of men and women in society, with both parents taking greater responsibility for childcare and home. As women have made great changes in life patterns, joining the male-dominated workplace in vast numbers over the last three decades, men have not yet made similar changes towards joining women in the nurturing rôle in great numbers. Our sons are the hope for the future as we condition their expectations of family life. In the meantime, we are still trying to 'do it all' with little help from partners, employers or society.

Banishing guilt

Is it easier to fight guilt if you can recognise it for what it is? I think so. In her book, *Necessary Losses*, Judith Viorst explains, 'True guilt . . . is the fear of our conscience's wrath, the loss of its love.' She goes on to demonstrate that excessive guilt or 'indiscriminate guilt' is the failure to distinguish between forbidden thoughts and forbidden deeds. This is going over the top, blaming yourself for the slightest thing. Equally excessive is 'omnipotent guilt', when our sense of being at fault is based on the illusion that we are in control, or could have or should have done something to affect a situation. 'If I had done that (or not done that) it would not have happened. . . . If I hadn't gone to work . . .' say scores of women each day. This is not surprising when they have been brainwashed into believing that it is all down to them, that every aspect of their family's wellbeing depends on mum.

Some guilt arises because it is seen as a deserved punishment from above for some act or omission. Take the example of the person who feels it is somehow her fault that her child is ill. It is sent to punish her for leaving him and going out to work. This self-flagellation is sadly too common. Several women told me of cases where a child was injured in a motor accident soon after the mother had returned to work. They did not say it was when the child was old enough to begin walking home alone, obviously a dangerous moment for any child wherever his mother is, or when he was allowed to walk across a road by another adult – true facts in two cases, but both mothers only linked the accident with their decision to work.

A healthy conscience produces guilt feelings appropriate to the so-called crime, but factors often combine to push this off-balance, and a neurotic conscience gets things out of proportion. Can we aim to assess coolly and calmly what is an appropriate response to events in our lives? How to retain a rational perspective is the 60-million-dollar question with no slick answer as it is so dependent on our overall mental health and balance.

A new perspective

Fortunately, there are signs of change as it becomes accepted that mothers work. As new norms emerge, women experience less conflict over their choices. Working mothers are still acknowledging guilt feelings but learning to build a new lifestyle to suit themselves. 'Women seem to be under pressure to be supermums/careerists, superwives and supersexy with superdress sense and supercars, just like the ad-men's Utopia. I have given up feeling guilty about it all and my [lack of] housework, and realised that I need time for Me and have started playing the piano again! You have to try to learn how to ignore guilt when it rears its ugly head, otherwise you go mad,' writes Kirsten.

'You have to fight hard to keep guilt at bay in lots of aspects of your life,' says Geraldine Hughes. 'So long as my children and I are reasonably happy, then I refuse to feel guilty about aspects which are missing in our lives. I don't have time to feel guilty. I think it is important to always try and see things in perspective. Guilt is niggling away but you must always try and keep it in check.'

Child-minder Kathy Hemmings can see guilt coming from all sides: 'Most people try to make you feel guilty about something at some point in the relationship with you. My mother says I don't phone enough, my children that I am not always there at school functions . . . It's no good feeling guilty – just work out the best thing for you, and do that thing on that day.'

Teacher Dyann Rowe has put it in its place 'As I get older, I feel I can cope with any guilt feelings much better. I adopt a "life's too short" attitude.'

Polly Toynbee thinks guilt is about how you are feeling about your own life. 'You need to analyse when you feel most guilty. Are the times when you suddenly think, "Oh, my God, I'm destroying my child, I must give it up," almost always when you yourself are under unbearable stress rather than when the child is? It's your own feelings rather than those of your child. If you've had a really hard day and things have gone badly at work, you think, "This is pointless, what am I doing wasting my time toiling away in an office churning out these little bits of news that'll be forgotten?" Come home and you'll think, "Oh, my poor baby, what have I done to you?" It's really about yourself. Times when you feel great, the job's going well, everything is all organised and you think – my child's terrific too, and it's all right.'

In her study *Growing Up in a Dual Career Family, The Children's Perception*, Patricia Knaub says, 'The most important thing parents can do is not approach their working with guilt. I've found over and over again that dual-career families often try to create a lifestyle as nearly like the traditional one as possible because they are feeling guilty. They don't really enlist the kids as often as they could and should in creating a new family structure. But, if the parents were to say to the children, "This is really a good way to live," a kid will believe it.'

Doing what you can

There is the notion, ingrained in us from the earliest age, that if a thing is not worth doing well it is not worth doing at all. This haunts overstressed working mums as they constantly realise they are not performing on all cylinders in every sphere of their lives. They have to reprogramme their thinking and allow a new dogma to take over: 'Do what you can.'

The very idea that you can do something well enough but not

perfectly is alien to achievers. Not doing your best 100 per cent of the time seems unthinkable. But is this a barrier to adventure and innovation? Does it stop you in your tracks when you think of attempting something new because you might not be able to do it perfectly? I know children who refuse to ride bicycles or learn to ski because they think they will not be able to do it well, or know that they do not excel at it. I know adults who are scared to try in case they make a fool of themselves. Remove the diktat that you must do everything well and a great deal more becomes possible. You can even be a 'good enough parent', say Bruno Bettelheim and Donald Winnicott – there are no perfect parents.

Once you come to terms with that, you feel a lot less guilty about not measuring up to some invisible standard of perfection; you stop reading features in women's magazines about improving yourself and making a new you. You realise that if you were to become the great cook that the recipe pages imply you should be, then you would not be the slim shape that the beauty pages idolise. You cannot be perfect at everything. Maybe you can be satisfied with yourself as you are.

You are going to have to choose. Aim for the top where it really matters and aim for a good enough level where it does not. This means sorting out priorities. You naturally want excellence in your communication with your children, with your partner and in your work, but you don't have to be the best cake sale cake-baker on the block. It means learning to say you cannot do the driving to the school sports event, it means diverting your energy to the human needs when you come home rather than slaving to make your home glossy-magazine perfect. It may mean bringing home a bunch of fresh flowers to give delight and freshen up the house when you have not had time to polish every surface.

It also means admitting you cannot do everything, and asking for help. Many mothers confirmed that they seldom asked their children for this. When Kay's mother asked her why she did not ask her children for more help she said of her daughter, 'She'll have to do it all her life. There's plenty of time for her to learn later.' It had not occurred to her to ask her son to do his share either. Could this be guilt-produced in some women? They feel guilty at leaving their homemaking rôle and retain it, rather than ask for help.

It is important to realise that children often *enjoy* being given responsibility. If your child feels badly let down by not having a cake for school events, for example, why not teach him to make a cake-mix cake at the earliest opportunity? I found this worked at nine, and no child was prouder than my son when he carried in his fabulous towering glossy chocolate extravaganza made by himself. Other mums' cakes paled in comparison. A valuable principle to keep in mind, says Kirsten, is one she learned while working at a Montessori Nursery School: 'Never do for a child what it can do for itself.'

For reducing guilt

Just as there were guilt-inducing ingredients in our 'soup', so there are guilt-reducing ones. To sum up then, here is a ten-point plan for dealing with guilt:

- Recognise and understand your guilt feelings
- Aim for a 'healthy' conscience
- Do not compare yourself to your mother or your husband's mother
- See 'the cult of motherhood' in perspective
- Set realistic standards
- Accept that you are going where few women have gone before
- Keep in mind the benefits your children gain from your working
- Set priorities
- Feel good about your dual-career life
- Forge new rôle models for the next generation

And, finally, always bear in mind the words of the song: 'Somebody's gotta hold back the river, but that somebody ain't you.'

Part Three

A changing society

'Get the piles off the floor, into the laundry baskets, Martin doesn't like mess.

'Creativity arises out of order not chaos. Five years off work while the children were small: back to work with seniority lost. What, did you think something was for nothing? If you have children, mother, that is your reward, it lies not in the world.'

Fay Weldon, 'Weekend' in *Watching Me Watching You* (1981)

HAVING BABIES AT 45 AND BEYOND

Single parents 'damage pupils'

Back to work

mother's ruin?

may groan at the
cliché – life begins
40 – but for many
ople it does signal a
me for drastic
anges of direction.

The changing shape of the family

'There's no vocabulary
For love within a family, love that's lived in
But not looked at . . .'

from *The Elder Statesman* by T.S. Eliot

Seeking this love and emotional satisfaction is a powerful drive for most of us. This much is unchanged. But the big news is the change in the shape of the groups in which we do this.

The nuclear family, upon which so much political thinking and product advertising is based, is undergoing a radical change. There is a shifting and a regrouping and what amounts to a weakening of traditional family patterns. There is a widening gap between the ideal and the reality – the way people think family life ought to be lived and how it actually is.

At first glance this seems to show a breakdown in relationships, but change does not mean the end of the family – many of the alternative family groupings offer stable and secure homes. As Sue Slipman says, 'The lesson from the UK is that family trends develop as individual liberty and personal responsibility evolve. The family as a form is neither dead nor dying – but it is changing.' A report by the Institute for Public Policy Research (IPPR), entitled *The Family Way*, also stressed how family structures evolve in response to social change: 'Families are social not natural phenomena, like the fall of snow in winter or the blossoming of trees in spring. They change over time, they are susceptible to and shaped by economic and political developments.'

Research supports these views. Figures from the Henley Centre for Forecasting show that one in three new marriages is destined for the rocks; one in five children has divorced parents by age 16; one in four children is born out of wedlock; and more than one million parents are bringing up children on their own.

Marriage as such is still popular. Marriages in England and Wales, which totalled 352,000 in 1989, are projected to fall only slightly in the year 2000 to 346,000. What has changed, however, is what happens within these households. Although 90 per cent of us still choose to marry and three-quarters of us live in households headed by couples, only 5 per cent of families in Britain consist of what has been thought of as the 'typical family' shown in the advertisements – father going out to work, mum staying home (getting her sheets whiter than white) and two children.

Although the number of babies born outside marriage is rising – it is expected to become one in three by 2000 – these are increasingly born into stable relationships. Many of the births are now registered by both parents who, in 7 out of 10 cases, are living at the same address. To show the rate of change in these figures, consider that in 1961, 38 per cent of such births were registered by both parents and in 1987 it had risen to 68 per cent.

Other research shows that 56 per cent of parents felt that there was nothing wrong in a woman regarding her job as important as her family; paradoxically, however, 55 per cent also agreed that raising a family ought to be more important to a woman than her job. Most people cite the family as their main source of satisfaction.

In the UK in 1990, there were 617,000 single parents on social security. Given incentives and help with childcare costs, they represent a huge potential workforce.

New models for the family

The old traditional family shape popular for more than a century and a half, the model of a Victorian middle-class family, projected as the ideal, is fading. For one thing it was based on the concept of one breadwinner and one carer, plus children. Respectability, a notion we hardly hear of today, was represented by a system of values for family life which was held up as the norm. Battles for higher wages were based on the concept of a man having to earn a wage that could support his family.

Instead of one model for the family unit, several different ones are now evolving. There are a greater number of single-parent families, and more serial monogamy with couples going into a subsequent marriage after the breakdown of the former. There are more 'amalgamated families' of half brothers and sisters, step fathers and mothers; there are new rôles for men and women as some men do more childcare and hordes of women find themselves the sole provider for a family; there are unmarried couples forming permanent households. This, then, is how we go into the last decade of the twentieth century.

One of the most important aspects of these changing patterns is that many more women are now working, for a number of reasons. In response to the survey in *Good Housekeeping* magazine women explained why they worked:

66 per cent said they work because they need the money
46 per cent said they wanted to pursue their careers
61 per cent said they liked the companionship and the interest
14 per cent cited other reasons

Although the idea of large numbers of women going out to work is relatively new, interestingly the concept of having someone else care for your child is not. It was prevalent among the aristocracy and later the upper classes, spreading to the middle classes and now to working women in general. There has been a long tradition of child rearers, trained or untrained, in this country.

9

The New Man

'The 90s will finally see the end of male machismo in favour of a new male role model, the loving caring family man and father,' stated the *Guardian* in 1990. Despite such claims, however, has anything really changed? Is the New Man just a figment of media imagination?

'I can bring home the bacon, fry it up in a pan, and never, never, never let you forget you're a man,' went an advertisement in 1978 for Enjoli perfume. And that is exactly what she did. Late-Seventies woman joined her mate as an earnings contributor, but she still went on cooking the meals, caring for the kids and ironing the shirts. More than a decade later, men's aversion to housework remains, while even their dominance in do-it-yourself skills is being threatened by women waving paint rollers.

It seems that women have been joining men, but men have been unchanging. Statistics chart the number of women who 'have joined men in the workplace' (women make up over 40 per cent of the workforce), but fail to examine how many men are sharing the nurturing with their partners. Children's needs, meanwhile, have not dwindled just because Mum is joining Dad in the outside world, so who will fill the care gap? There are some men who have stepped into the gap and taken on a fair share of childcare, but the New Man has not turned out to be as universal as predicted.

What surveys find

The Annual British Attitudes Survey reports gender rôles unbendingly rigid in the home: the woman still prepares the evening meal in 77 per cent of households; she does the cleaning in 72 per cent and the washing and ironing in 88 per cent.

A special report by *Under 5* magazine found that 70 per cent of men never do ironing or dusting. One in seven male partners never help with shopping. Only 30 per cent of male partners get up at night if children cry. Only a third of fathers dished out the discipline and 50 per cent of mothers said the ultimate responsibility for the children's welfare falls on them. Less than half said that it was shared. Two out of three mothers made decisions about the principles of their children's diet – which may affect their health and wellbeing for the rest of their lives.

According to the Henley Centre for Forecasting's *Planning for Social Change*, women without children have an average of 42 hours a week leisure time; women with children have a mere 22. For men, having children has little effect on the amount of free time they enjoy. Men without children have an average of 49 leisure hours a week, while men with children have 46.

In the USA, Professor Arlie Hochschild of Berkeley found a similar picture. She chronicled the home lives of dual-career couples in her book entitled *The Second Shift*, conjuring up a scene of a wife slaving away at meals, mothering and menial tasks, while her spouse watches television. Hochschild divides men's attitudes to their working wives into three categories: traditional, transitional and egalitarian. It is the transitionals that one needs to be wary of – they talk big about equality but do little.

Nothing much has changed in the underlying structure of things within the four walls of the home. Despite the Pill, free love and feminism, women still do the chores – housework, laundry, shopping and childcare. Men change light bulbs, mow lawns and do a bit of DIY (although this is another field in which marketing research shows women coming up pretty fast).

Absentee fathers

Mothers who work are often blamed for the disintegration of family life – a mother's place is with her family, or the family will suffer, it is claimed. It seems, however, that Mum goes out to work, but that Dad is overworking. Men in Britain worked increasingly long hours during the Eighties (the longest hours in the EC, and with an increasing proportion as overtime), and many are forced by high property values to commute long distances to areas they can afford. This makes them absentee fathers.

Available briefly at the weekend, concerned but peripheral figures, they are poor rôle models for their sons. There is an argument that this lack of intimacy with the children on the part of fathers leads boys to develop rigid masculine rules and codes, and renders them less able to express their emotions. Heather Formaini, in her book *Men, The Darker Continent*, explains that a father's occasional help is not enough: 'I would like to see a situation where men and women share childrearing and also play an equal part in the outside world. I'd like to see a world where bringing up children is seen as a creative act and there is far less separation of public and private spheres.' Formaini explains that in single-parent families headed by a mother, 'boys don't grow up hearing women ridiculed, or seeing them as inferior to the male'. She takes the rather radical view that a father should either play a full rôle or get out altogether.

Unfortunately, as long as men earn so much more than women, it will not be possible for many couples to make fundamental changes in their hours of work without a major loss of income for the family. Then there is the question of attitudes and prejudices. More than two decades of women's liberation have brought women the right to open doors for themselves or buy a man lunch, but little has changed at home once the front door slams.

Where no man has gone before

There are over 11.5 million married women working in the UK, all possible candidates for a change in lifestyle towards more shared responsibility for home life. Yet, where couples do try to establish a new pattern, sharing household and childcare chores equally, they come up against the constraints of the workplace and its anti-family structure, and against social pressures that reveal society's lack of support and respect for childcare and for children. They report disapproval from all quarters – from workmates, from other mothers, from schools, and even from their own families.

Men attempting to take a greater rôle at home battle against long working hours and commuting time. They may have to take shift work or shorter hours, or lose out on promotional prospects. Childcare is still not seen as a macho activity. So they may find themselves under pressure from male workmates, friends and relatives. There is sometimes even disapproval from other women, suggesting that a man's partner is wrong to have him do this.

Dave told me that his boss is a childless woman who frowns on him leaving a meeting to fetch the kids, even if he is happy to return to work and work late. More than one man has described the difficult atmosphere at his place of work: 'It is assumed that if you want to get on you will work all hours. It isn't even really necessary, but if others are doing it it becomes the norm. You stand out if you leave early, you don't seem committed.'

Fathers doing their share talk of not being able to mention this side of their lives amongst their workmates and friends: 'I keep quiet about it, they wouldn't understand, they'd think I was a bit soft,' said Michael. A concern with relationships and caring in a male environment is still seen as a weakness rather than a human strength. One view is that to achieve power and success in the workplace you need to be less concerned with relationships, and you may even have to tread on others to get ahead. Love and nurturing will get you a corny card on Father's Day, but will not earn you a high score in the masculine world of work.

There are difficulties away from the workplace too. Dads taking a child to playgroup tell of awkwardness when they find another congenial parent (always a mother). If you ask her over to tea with her child what are the connotations? How will she take this? How will our partners take this? Many women are reluctant to build a friendship with such a father as they see him as another woman's partner. Will this mean your child has fewer invitations?

Being the only dad fetching children in a group of mothers does have its moments, though. Simon Jenkins, at the time of writing editor of *The Times* and an involved father, explained that he was occasionally the only parent to discipline a mob of unruly kids – the mothers seemed grateful.

Relatives often make one feel judged, too. Ann noticed her brother-in-law watching in amazement as her husband changed the baby's nappy expertly in the back of the car, and she idly wondered if people think she is incompetent because he does it?

Good – but not quite good enough

Learning to share is something mothers need to do, as well as fathers. For so long, women's identity has been bound up with giving birth and rearing children, and it can be hard to give up this identity – in doing so, we may feel that we no longer know who we are. Some mothers may find giving up their 'mothering power' easy and will feel '100 per cent confident in his ability', while others may feel a little displaced, or threatened if their partners show a real expertise in 'their' area of influence. Some say they simply do not have the confidence in their partner's ability and so could not hand the child over to him, or could not let go themselves. In subtle ways they may keep their partner at a distance from childcare tasks, underlining his lack of know-how or reliability, and so cling to their old identity.

Several men told me that although they do their share, say, of tidying up the house, women still redo a lot of the tasks. Mark, an academic who is often working at home, told me that he will tidy up with anyone who is home, a child perhaps, but that when his wife, a busy solicitor, comes in, she will go round plumping up cushions and re-arranging things.

Danielle, a child psychoanalyst, told me that, although her husband may do his share in the kitchen, she always has an urge to wipe the sink as he does not do it the same way she does. These gestures can be seen as a means of reclaiming territory – of marking the place almost as an animal might do. Whether or not the family and *au pair* have tidied up, there are women who still want to add their touch in some small way. In doing so, they are not saying that the initial tidying has not been done well, they are simply adding their little bit, making it their home once again and putting their stamp on it. If this is misunderstood, many a tentative effort to be New Man is foiled. A man will retreat, thinking it is a criticism of his contribution. A frank discussion about this may clear the air.

In praise of fathers

'It is time to dethrone the idea that Real Men are aggressive, loud, competitive, unemotional, unexpressive and irresponsible, and begin to shape a concept of Real Men as sensitive, concerned, tender and self-aware both in their dealings with each other and with women and children. In the recent past such figures have been dismissed as wimps and wets. But in the long run if civilisation is to survive and violence be contained it is the wimps and wets who must inherit the earth.'

Jeffrey Richards, Professor of Cultural History
at Lancaster University

Caring, involved fathers could signal the beginning of a major change as the next generation grows up with different expectations in a world where the male stereotype of achievement – favouring separateness of the individual as against connectedness with other – is no longer dominant. This male stereotype has tended to split work and love into male and female compartments, seeing a concern with relationships and sensitivity to the needs of others as a feminine characteristic, and in this way devaluing it. Yet some men have within them extraordinary powers for parenting, and feel enriched and 'in touch' through this close and intimate contact with their families. Mothers speak glowingly of them:

'He's brilliant with her, so natural.'

'He's more in touch with the child in himself and knows how to play with the baby, which I find more difficult.'

'I have total confidence in him as far as the children are concerned.'

'I could never have managed without my husband's help.'

'He brings another way of looking at things to the decisions we make about childrearing.'

'He's much more adventurous with the children. He makes them less fearful, more ready to tackle the world.'

Fathers who 'only come out at night', in novelist Margaret Atwood's words, find it much more difficult to relate to children they have never been alone with much. If a marriage breaks up they may have difficulty in keeping a relationship going with kids. (In half of all divorces fathers lose contact with their children within two years.)

Comparing young and old

In the shifting trends in home life, it is interesting to compare the experiences of older and younger couples. Younger couples report more sharing of home tasks, but this may change as they become parents. If the woman stays home for a period, they usually feel the loss of her earnings and the man may work harder and longer to compensate. Then, because she is at home, she will gradually take on more of the domestic tasks, such as having a meal ready for him when he returns. Couples say this is when a gradual return to traditional rôles begins to creep in. Dad may now help with the children in his free time but he slowly relinquishes housework.

Older couples report interesting changes, however. Maureen and her husband have grown children in their twenties. She has worked, initially part-time, but over the last few years has taken on more and more until she is now in a position of great responsibility: 'I run a hospital,' she says. She commutes into London from Billericay and then has a tube journey across the city. This means that she is home late every evening. Her husband has adapted and has the dinner on when she gets back, and helps generally. Maureen explains that while she worked part-time and locally he never saw the need to do this.

One family's story

Karen and Andy have made a definite decision to run their lives on an equal, sharing basis and they hope to bring up their children in a non-sexist way. Shiftwork for Andy and teachers' hours and holidays for Karen enable couples like them to do this. They also need the minimum outside help with the children. Karen commutes into London where she runs a nursery class, and Andy works a rotating shift nearer home. By taking shiftwork, he recognises that he is sidelined for promotion.

Their most difficult time is the early morning before school starts, but they havè found that a dinner lady at school will keep the children with her and take them into school. Andy mostly collects them and gives them tea, and also shops for groceries and does the laundry. He is the parent most available for visits to school events and meets other parents in the afternoons at the school gate. He comments that this pattern was acceptable in London when they lived in Hackney, but he is regarded as distinctly odd now that they live in a small Essex village where gender rôles are clear and traditional.

Karen complains of criticism from other women who do not hesitate to tell her she is doing the wrong thing, despite the fact that her youngest child has a place in the nursery and is with her all day. Both parents report difficulties, too, in allowing the children to cross gender barriers and do whatever activities they would like to. No girls play football here, no boys do ballet, so these budding stars of field and stage are relegated to more conventional activities. Chess and country dancing are just two more of the activities with a gender bias they have found.

Despite his enormous contribution to housework and childcare, Andy sees himself as the supporting player, ultimately deferring to Karen in childcare. He says she has the right to decide major questions of 'policy', and she needs to keep her role as primary carer and mother, which is how she wants to see it. Andy thinks that this reflects reality because Karen has a teacher's training and some knowledge of psychology. On certain issues he will suggest to the children they 'wait and ask Mummy when she comes home'.

Of course, this does mean that Karen and Andy contradict one another at times, as Andy admitted: 'We still bang up against each other occasionally . . . I let them do this and she has said the previous day on no account can they do it. We have to be aware they don't manipulate us, but I don't think it affects them adversely.'

Although Andy is responsible for the laundering, it is Karen who decides what they will wear. This is part of her mothering control and is a remnant of the time when she worked around the children's school hours and carried all the responsibility for them.

Letting go of this total responsibility can be a difficult process for a mother who has at first been at home all the time and later, part-time. In Karen's case, however, she will be home with the children throughout the school holidays, when she can retrieve her central rôle.

How to encourage the New Man

Fathers cannot become New Men if mothers do not learn to share mothering. This will include allowing your partner to make mistakes and 'learn on the job' – something which is difficult to tolerate, especially in a household under pressure. It has to be understood that it is acceptable for him to do things a little differently from you. The baby, after all, has not read the rule book. I particularly remember my own husband sitting feeding our baby and holding him only by the armpits so that his body dangled down between my husband's knees. There was none of the correct cradling and support of the head. I was about to open my mouth to say something but noticed just in time that the baby was glugging down the bottle with no signs of dissatisfaction.

Clearly mothers need to learn how to draw out a partner's potential for parenting, encouraging him to develop this alongside them from the start. They need to learn how to greet fathers at the school gate instead of 'freezing them out' with an icy stare. They need to learn to support 'equal sharing' couples without criticism, implied or spoken.

We also need a change in the relationship between work and family, so that men's caring abilities are recognised and policy makers are urged to create a new framework to enable both women *and* men to meet their family responsibilities.

10

Single parents

The family has shown itself vulnerable to change and we are living through a period in which we see evidence of this all around us. The ever-rising divorce figures since the divorce reforms of 1959 are expected to continue upward, and today one in five children will experience their parents' separation before the age of 16. The proportion of births outside wedlock has reached one in four, and one in six families is now headed by a single parent. There are 1.1 million such parents in the UK, 90 per cent of whom are women. Nearly 70 per cent depend on welfare benefits and, on average, the one-parent family has 37 per cent of the income of the two-parent family. These families face major problems of poverty and, according to Sue Slipman of the National Council for One Parent Families, 'because of the way our benefit system works, one-parent families are being pushed into an underclass at society's margins, with the risk that their children will be cut off from any ladder of opportunity'. Policy makers can no longer ignore the problems faced by single parents and their children, as they struggle to escape what has become a poverty trap.

In the UK, among lone mothers of children under five, only 7 per cent work full time, compared with 27 per cent in West Germany, 44–49 per cent in France, Belgium and Italy, and 50 per cent in Denmark.

When deciding whether or not to work, a lone mother in Britain faces different problems from those of a mother in a two-parent household. The loss of benefit, when set against the low earnings in part-time work for which the majority opt, does not make working worthwhile if a mother has to pay for childcare. Then there are the additional costs of working, such as transport and clothing. The lone parent is caught in a trap unless the work she can get really pays.

The campaigns of the National Council for One Parent Families have altered from the initial emphasis on improving benefit, to one in which the aim is to get people trained and ready for work that ideally pays adequately. Sue Slipman is adamant: 'Lone parents have to be helped to become financially independent through work if we are not to face dire consequences for their children and escalating public expenditure and other costs for society as a whole. Moreover, women's aspirations have genuinely changed: they are not going to be pushed back into the home.'

A cause of delinquency and crime?

Lone parents are often blamed for delinquency rates and other social problems of the young but 'there is no evidence to support the idea that lone parenthood is in itself a direct cause of under-achievement of children, juvenile delinquency, crime or general social disintegration,' reports the Institute for Public Policy Research in its paper *The Family Way*.

The paper reported that there were two factors often associated with lone parenthood which may cause problems: changing relationships and poverty. Children of divorced parents, it went on, 'may experience trauma, loss and insecurity, which may have a detrimental effect on their development'. There are so many factors which can vary in every case: whether the absent father remains in close touch or not; whether the children form attachments to other adults; whether secure relationships are maintained; and whether stimulating interaction is provided.

Children can, of course, be insecure and emotionally deprived in two-parent families, and there is evidence that they can be as emotionally healthy in one-parent families as in conventional ones. But it is well documented that lone parenthood and, in particular, lone motherhood, is associated with poverty. Only 19 per cent of lone parents own their own houses compared with 67 per cent of two-parent families, according to a study by Jo Roll.

The struggle to balance childcare and a part-time job often results in stress and the mother may be no better off working than she would on benefits. The difficulties faced by many children of these families closely match those of children in low-income groups. *The Family Way* concludes that lone parenthood is often associated with material deprivation, and continues, 'we also learn that material deprivation is often linked to such problems as juvenile delinquency and educational under-achievement'. But the authors forcefully conclude that 'to argue that lone parenthood is therefore a cause of delinquency or under-achievement is an affront to reason, not unlike shooting the messenger'.

Freedom and responsibility

'There's a large measure of freedom which is often absent in a relationship with a partner,' writes Diana, single mother and air stewardess on short-haul flights. 'You don't have to have anyone's permission to do anything explicit or implicit.'

When things get busy and stressed, Diana, like so many of those I interviewed, lets housework slide: 'But then I have only myself to please, and Harriet. No man or others to satisfy.' The choices are hers alone – she will do the washing but can live without ironing. She believes it is vital to keep up bedtime stories and a relaxing bathtime, which she sees as 'bonding time and educational, too, lots of secrets exchanged at bathtime and imagination time for all'.

Hazel, who works as a teacher and has had many more years of single parenting, describes the endless work pressure of being a single earner. 'As a single parent I feel so alone in all this. If I stop working, then there is no income except for the ridiculous child support. For the past year I have suddenly felt so swamped under the constant strain of supporting us. Because there's a terribly relentless, vicious circle involved.'

She describes the 'burn out' typical among teachers. Hazel finds herself unable to retrain because of the cost and the lack of income that it would require. 'So, in order to make life less tedious I spoil myself with things like music and holidays, and to compensate Karen for living in a grotty flat in a grotty area, I let her buy the things she wants – but of course extra luxuries mean extra money so I have to take on an extra job or more teaching hours. So I feel even more burnt out.'

For Hazel, the stress of sole responsibility is balanced by the freedom to parent as she sees fit, and by the rewarding nature of her relationship with her lovely daughter of 17. She is quite definite on this, and to see them together is to realise how happy they are in each other's company. 'Despite the endless pressure and work dissatisfaction, I have never regretted not being able to study or retrain because being Karen's mother has been a marvellous, rewarding, life-giving experience,' she says. 'I have the preciousness of a one-to-one relationship as well as total control in the positive sense, i.e. I don't have to compromise my ideas of parenting. I can always do what I think is best for Karen and I get so much love, and it's me she tells the daily things to, and it's me who gets to share in all the laughter . . .'

To be the sole recipient of the good times is wonderful but there are times when being on your own is much less fun – when the worries predominate and there is no partner with whom to share them. 'I have to cope with all decisions alone,' says Hazel. 'And if she's sad and lets me in I have no one to share my worries with. I often think that single parenting is so tough because it is so alone. . . . However, two parents don't always agree on decisions, so I'm free of strife there.'

There are those who say that they probably spend more time with their children because they are single parents than they would if they were married or living with a partner. But this may not always be out of choice. Social life for many simply comes to a halt: 'You've only got to say you have a three-year-old for men to melt away.' With financial constraints coming high on the list of disincentives, finding someone to look after the children is difficult for many, so that they are not able to get out much on their own.

So, for lone parents, there is a weighing-up to be done with, on the one hand, the freedom of being able to do things your way and, on the other, the immense responsibility of providing emotional, financial and simply companionable support for children. There is also the question of your own need for support, companionship, and time for leisure and social activities. As Sue Slipman explains: 'You absolutely have to confront your own psychology of dependence when you have a child, because raising a child with one pair of hands is incredibly difficult and demanding. I'm a very strong person and at times I'm on the ropes. I can't cope with this. There are hard times when you have no choice. You have to make it work. But it is an emotional test of you and I think it must be extremely difficult not to, in some way, visit that on the child. But we seem to pull through and there's so much joy involved that it's a massive compensation.'

Single out of choice

Although this group is small, it is growing as women feel more able to cope with single parenthood alone. In some cases, this may be because a woman is financially secure and it may sometimes reflect the age of the mother – an independent, self-supporting woman reaching her forties may feel that time is running out on her.

Judith found herself in just this position. After many years working for Christian Aid all over the world, she began to take stock of her life: 'I was rushing about trying to turn this world into a better place – I hadn't even sorted myself out,' she says. Judith felt she wanted an ongoing relationship with people in her work, not simply addressing meetings and rushing off, so she switched to teaching. Gradually she came to understand her wish to have her own child. She watched a close friend parenting alone, and observed: 'She thinks this is the best thing she's ever done. Her daughter is delightful, extraordinarily self-aware, integrated, an independent small girl. I saw how it could be a very fulfilling thing for her and the child didn't seem to suffer.'

Judith chose single parenthood knowing from the start that her partner would not stay in the UK. She has a good relationship with the child's father though he lives abroad. She does not depend on him financially at all. As a first time mother at 40, she feels exhausted and says: 'Physicallly it has been a killer. The pain of being physically shattered, however, is nothing to that emotional desert. What a huge hole there was in my life.' She has returned to teaching and has a place for her daughter in a crêche, but is considering other forms of childcare.

A way forward

So are single mothers finding it all much more difficult than they thought? The answers are as diverse as the make-up of the individuals concerned. For some this was a challenge to prove themselves: 'My career has taken off since the break-up. It was as if I was playing at making a living before.' Riva's determination to get ahead has her working at her job and studying for her master's degree while raising three children. 'I have my own tremendous career drive. I am determined to succeed.'

Sue Slipman acknowledges the importance of confidence: 'Our approach is about enabling them to become competent individuals. If you're a competent person you feel confident, and you're likely to mother more competently. Our approach is a holistic one.' She is very hopeful about retraining schemes offered through polytechnic and local authorities. Thanks to intense lobbying, there is now £50.00 a week available in childcare costs for someone who ha been on income support and is into a training scheme. Other ideas include tax concessions for a childcare voucher scheme, and a research project is under way to determine who needs this, where they are and how the scheme can be administered.

Sue points out that when you accept that you are a lone parent, and are not continually seeking the traditional way out via remarriage, you are free to make arrangements for your life, such as sharing your house with another single-parent family as she does. However, to do this 'you have to confirm that you are single rather than think "Someday my Prince will come".' The arrangement Sue has made has many pluses. The two mothers share a house, enabling them to have better accommodation than they would otherwise. They share aspects of childcare and the children have one another as siblings, since 'neither of us is likely to have another child'.

Increasingly single-parent families and new 'post-nuclear' family groupings are gaining recognition. The mother and child unit is a fundamental icon. As agony aunt Claire Rayner put it: 'The only real family unit at its most basic and biological is the mother and child.' We will be seeing more of these mother and child units.

A new life at 40

The week my eldest strode off to his first job, my neighbour, not much younger than I, produced her first baby. This extraordinary difference in the experience of women roughly the same age highlights some of the new and astonishing changes in women's health and aspirations.

Modern health care, increased life expectancy and efficient contraception have changed the shape of generations. No longer do women expect to marry and have children in their twenties, see them grow up by their forties and go back to work, face the empty nest syndrome at 50 and become graceful grandmas at 60. The old pattern is disintegrating: stages, not ages, is the theme.

The choices facing women often come to a head at the age of 40. A 40-year-old woman, free after many years of the responsibility of children, can now expect a long and healthy working life. At the same time, a woman of the same age who has worked for most of her adult life may still decide to have a baby, often delaying until her fortieth birthday and sometimes even later.

Traditionally, reaching 40 was the time when you gave up any ideas of major life changes, and prepared yourself to settle into comfortable middle age. But modern women do not seem to feel this way. The message from many older first-time mothers was, 'I don't feel old. When my mother was my age she seemed somehow different, elderly.' It seems that women in mid-life today are ready to tackle new jobs, new studies, new partners and even new babies. The ripe old age of 40 is now a time of growth and challenge, a time when women take stock. They ask: 'Is this all there is?' 'Can I do something else before it is too late?' 'How will I solve the working/parenting dilemma?' and 'Is this my last chance to have a child?'

The present shortage of school-leaving-age children may attest to this generation's move into careers. Large numbers of successful 40-year-olds in careers are childless today. Although the baby boom of the early Nineties shows some new thinking on the part of younger women, it also includes a large number of older women who have waited until their late thirties or early forties to have a child.

These women were young in a fluid moment in time when expectations and reality for women did not yet converge. 'We found ourselves encouraged to try to have it all, have a satisfying career on equal terms with men, while at the same time enjoying a rich and loving personal life. It was all made to sound easy and within reach.' As the Eighties have ended and they reach '40-something', what is the real state of play?

A matter of timing

According to Joanna Foster of the Equal Opportunities Commission, and herself a mother, the typical pattern that women's lives have taken on is that of a 'patchwork', made up of working and mothering periods drawn together to form a whole. The patches are made up of stretches of work, career breaks, new directions and returns to work; in contrast, men's career structures tend to be linear. What has emerged as the major issue for many women is not deciding whether or not to work, but choosing when and if a family life could be supported alongside a job – a decision most men never face.

Broadly, women fall into two groups: those who have decided to have children early and turn to work when the children have gone; and those who have put career first, and opted for motherhood later. Women in the first group, who had children in their early twenties, are seeing them grow into young men and women now, leaving mums free to tackle new careers, mid-life changes, and adjust to new freedoms after years of parental responsibility. You might call this the 'kids first, work second' group.

Frequently women in this group have retrained or added a qualification during their children's school years and are ready to try out a new phase of their careers, or indeed, a new career altogether. Vivienne and Arlene, for example, have gained law degrees and began to work in law firms where youngsters who had already been there a couple of years were senior to them.

Tanya, with one child in university and another finishing his schooling, has gone back to studying and is teaching mentally handicapped children as part of her course. Maureen has brought up her children and moved from part-time administration work into a full-time post running a hospital. Other women tackled the work/family life issue the other way round. The 'work first, motherhood later' group are having their first babies now. These first-time mothers, in their late thirties or just 40, form a substantial and rapidly growing group whose numbers have doubled in 10 years. They talk of finding life so 'interesting, stimulating and full' that they did not feel ready to think of starting a family before. 'I wanted nothing to interfere with my work,' is another comment I heard.

However, as they approached the seeming barrier of 40, with all the risks that age now implies for first-time mothers, they talk of feeling the lack of a child very strongly. Some describe this as Biopanic or a pre-menopausal fling, but it seems nearer the truth to see it as a consequence of trying to fulfil complex female needs. Liz, an art teacher and illustrator, explains, 'I'd explored other aspects of what I could do with my life and couldn't bear to think I wouldn't have a child of my own, and with 40 coming up . . .'

Suzanne had her first child at 40 after devoting years to building a successful business in classic cars with her husband. 'Once I became pregnant, I never had the slightest doubt about this new step. There was not one second when I didn't want it.' She says she realised then how much she had wanted this 'in my heart but was afraid to admit it to myself'.

Suzanne suggested other reasons for women delaying motherhood: 'I think there are probably more older first-time mothers in the cities because there is an exciting life for which you need freedom. Then, buying any sort of home and getting set up is so expensive, it takes longer for a couple to be able to settle down together.' Indeed many remain committed to a career and never 'settle down'.

She also points out that, at 40, some of us lose a parent and 'with the loss of someone close to you, you begin to realise that you need loving relationships around you. Life is renewed through another generation and, through the child, you look towards the future rather than back towards the grief.'

Waiting game

Taking the decision to try and start a family in their late thirties was certainly a major step, but it was only the first hurdle: all the mothers I spoke to told of frustrating waits before they fell pregnant. For Suzanne, this was a time when she tried to adjust to the idea that she might never have children, and she looked for other compensations such as travel. Liz, having decided that she finally wanted a baby, remembers friends asking her why she chose to work with children if it only made her longing for her own child more acute. They felt she was putting herself through extra heartache. Bea, who miscarried when the longed-for child was expected, had to overcome an emotional crisis before she could begin again.

All understood that there was a greater risk in a first pregnancy at this age. The risk of Down's Syndrome rises from less than one in 1500 live births in mothers aged 20–30 to one in 130–150 live births in mothers aged 40–44. These extra worries accompanied the decision and the pregnancy. Once the relief of the baby's arrival had passed, further hurdles lay ahead.

Magnificently unprepared . . .

Adjusting to the new 24-hour job of motherhood made great demands on women who had led lives in which they had not been tied down in any way for close on 20 adult years. Nor were they helped in this by the Eighties emphasis on personal achievement, self-gratification and assertiveness in the marketplace. Mothering requires just the opposite – a certain amount of selfless giving and of putting oneself second to the needs of the baby. For most mothers, there is a great deal of learning involved in becoming a parent, but for these women, in particular, it came as a shock. Competent and efficient career women suddenly found themselves all at sea, floundering with no know-how and totally exhausted.

One of the difficulties for them lay in the fact that their identity had been tied up with their careers: 'For me, my work isn't just my profession,' said Anne, writer and broadcaster, 'it's part of my identity. It's not just a job I go in and do and go home . . . it's such a very important part of my sense of self I express through my work.' She added that, after investing in a career for so long, 'the loss [of giving it up] is greater than for a secretary in her twenties'.

Liz said that, despite having wanted for so long to have a baby, she found it difficult 'being so disabled by the physical need of this child and the attention he needed'. She added that she felt bad about this and guilty about 'feeling chained down'.

Fatigue is a major problem for all mothers. 'Why didn't anybody tell me!' said Annette, as she struggled to get over the exhaustion and sense of overwhelming responsibility in the early weeks. But is tiredness greater for the older group? Anne thought not: 'In my twenties I would sleep nine or 10 hours a night. I could never have managed on this amount of sleep, either emotionally or physically then.'

The shock of the responsibility hits home too: 'That's the feeling, the responsibility, I feel sick . . . with the responsibility.' Maturity does not seem to be much of a help in coping with it either. 'In theory, one has greater patience and maturity,' said one mother. 'For all that, I have felt desperate, absolutely desperate . . . I mean I think there are things that I wouldn't have been able to cope with 10 years, even five years ago. I feel as if I may be 39 but I was never really grown up, I was playing at life. This is a real dose of reality and it's more than I can bear.'

Because of their maturity, younger women in ante-natal classes seemed to expect these older mums-to-be to know more about childbirth and childcare. Liz, however, said she felt 'equally naive'. Bea spoke of two distinct groups at her hospital classes: 'There were the very young girls in their late teens, and then a large group of us over-35s with nothing in-between. We had absolutely nothing in common. The older women had careers and experience, the younger ones wanted to talk about hairstyles.'

How had parenthood changed these women? All expressed deep emotional responses to their babies and noted major changes in their attitudes to life, making comments such as: 'It turns you upside down, every preconceived notion goes out of the window'; 'I always knew it intellectually, but now I know it emotionally, it's the hardest thing in the whole world and the most difficult challenge I ever had'; 'It's the complete opposite of the life I knew. After the companionship at work, I now feel everything is down to me and I'm conscious of being alone in this.'

'I had quite firm ideas about childrearing and wanted to do it differently from the way my mother did it, and then suddenly I find myself a total incompetent. I can't do it at all, let alone well, and with no time for myself and no time for my partner, the shock is dreadful from all these losses.'

There were positive responses, too. Liz remarked, 'I am more aware of my own health, battling to give up smoking and looking after myself better, as I am responsible for this chap.' Suzanne said it had changed her view of the world now that she had a child who would inherit it. 'Overall I would say it has been a 95 per cent positive experience. I was flagging a bit before . . .' is a common view from women who had tried out many variations on living before motherhood. All intended to continue working, although part time or freelance at first.

Building a whole

Both groups of mothers, early or late, approach the coming years trying to bring all the facets of our complex female selves into a satisfying whole. There are new responsibilities ahead. Forecasts indicate that we will all be called upon to care for an older generation and we expect to be working. Both groups of mothers – early and late – have much in common as we continue to try to make a dual contribution of caring and working . . . it is a little daunting, though, to realise that by the time the later group of mothers are dealing with adolescent kids, those who tackled parenthood first may be answering to cries of 'Grandma!'

Part Four

Care

'Children are very resilient to the ups and downs of their various care-givers as long as their central relationship with their mother remains consistent. It is this important fact which the guilt-ridden, anxious, competitive new mothers who want to work should try to remember. Their relationship with the baby is unique and central to both the baby and themselves.'

Dr Jane Price, psychiatrist and psychotherapist,
Motherhood: What It Does to Your Mind (1988)

Family allowance

Women call for help in returning to work

Mummy Trap

Beware the nanny tr

Breaking up, not breaking down

Million women unable to work

12

Choosing care

'Childcare is grossly undervalued. It's a terrific responsibility to take on the upbringing of someone else's child. My mother has been staying with me and she didn't realise how hard I had to work at childminding – she never before realised it was a *job*,' said Kathy, a childminder. Most people do not see caring for children as a valid job in its own right, and Kathy's experience underlines this attitude.

People think that women mother automatically and instinctively. 'Motherhood is often seen as women's destiny. Whether they have children or are childless, women cannot escape being treated as mothers, whatever they make of their individual lives,' say Caroline New and Mirian David in *For the Children's Sake*. 'Women are given caring work on the grounds that they are mothers, or may become mothers, or should have been mothers. They are even expected to feel like mothers when they work as teachers, social workers, nurses or help out at playgroup and to be satisfied with no pay or low pay.'

It is only when we have to part with a precious baby – who is somehow already an individual – that we realise how hard it is to find someone with the special qualities needed to be a substitute mum. Matching your needs to a suitable carer proves to be one of the most difficult experiences you face as a working parent. Now you know that not just any motherly woman will do. The worry of finding someone suitable can be a great strain, eating into the precious weeks of maternity leave.

Facts and figures

The solutions we find to our childcare needs are varied, individually arranged and often consist of cobbled-together care arrangements. The *Good Housekeeping* survey gave some interesting insights into the kinds of childcare we choose, our attitudes to it – and also when we choose to return to work, a decision often closely affected by the types of care available, and the cost of it. What the respondents said is shown below:

Who looked after the children?

30 per cent used a nanny, childminder or au pair

29 per cent used a relative or friend, husband or partner

28 per cent said the children were at school until they were able to be with them

21 per cent said the children were old enough not to need supervision

Who should be responsible for providing childcare?

87 per cent felt the government does not do enough to help working mothers

63 per cent felt that women should be solely responsible for arranging their childcare

31 per cent thought that women should pay for it

When did mothers go back to work?

31 per cent returned straight after maternity leave

27 per cent returned when the child went to nursery school

30 per cent returned when the child went to primary school

Did age and location make a difference?

57 per cent of the under-35s returned to work immediately after maternity leave

25 per cent of 35- to 44-year-olds returned after maternity leave

40 per cent of mothers returning immediately lived in cities

26 per cent of mothers making an immediate return lived in rural areas

What were the effects of being back at work?

37 per cent took a cut in income

32 per cent reported a soul- and confidence-destroying lowering of status

The piecemeal services available in Britain add to the confusion when parents begin their search for childcare. Subsidised local authority nursery lists are full and very often places reserved for single parents' children or otherwise 'deprived' children. In the whole of Britain, there is 1.7 per cent provision for under-threes and 44 per cent for three- to five-year-olds, while Italy boasts 76 per cent, France 95 per cent and Belgium 96 per cent.

In February 1990, the study by Working for Childcare brought out figures for the country as a whole:

1 per cent of under-fives have places in local authority nurseries

20 per cent of three- to four-year-olds attend nursery schools and classes, but 83 per cent of places are part time

20 per cent of four-year-olds attend primary schools

4 per cent of under-fives are cared for by childminders

13 per cent of under-fives are cared for by playgroups, but most attend only two or three times per week and only 1 per cent of groups affiliated to the Preschool Playgroups Association operate hours which coincide with working hours. (One of the basics about attending a playgroup is that mothers do their share of helping out, an impossible requirement for a working mum.)

The study estimates that there are only 300 workplace nurseries in the whole of the UK. It also estimates that 44 per cent of children are cared for by relatives or grandmothers, offering no figure for nannies or au pairs. The Daycare Trust suggests that 3.3 per cent of under-fives are looked after by registered childminders, and 1.7 per cent by unregistered minders.

A survey conducted by Social and Community Planning Research and published in November 1991 revealed that although 51 per cent of the women surveyed were in favour of workplace nurseries, no working mothers with children under five in the survey were able to use this type of nursery care: 64 per cent used a relative, 24 per cent employed a nanny or childminder and only 9 per cent used a local authority nursery. When asked which additional options they would use if available, women employees with children under 12 favoured term-time working contracts (70 per cent) and school holiday care arrangements (48 per cent). However, the survey found that even if childcare and flexible working practices were more widely available, the predominant attitude among men – that women should be responsible for childcare arrangements – was likely to reinforce gender-based occupational segregation as men were unwilling to alter their working hours.

A Policy Studies Institute survey published in the same month covering 5000 women and 500 employers demonstrates a revolution in the position of working mothers. Almost 50 per cent of women who leave their jobs to have children are back at work full time or part time within nine months of giving birth.

When you start looking at the different options for care available in your area, your local social services area office should supply information about all registered services and all types of nurseries, as well as childminders and playgroups. But, with the diverse nature of childcare and the numerous organisations involved, trying to understand what is on offer in your area can be bewildering. What is available may not suit you either. The hours may not coincide with your work hours, and you may not be able to afford the fees of an extra carer to cover this.

Adequate childcare releases women for work, financial independence and greater equality. At the same time adequate childcare services assure the employer of a reliable worker. The answer is partnership between users, employers, and providers of care.

In a new scheme, employers are being asked to join in to create information services. In 1989, Childcare Links was set up as a pilot project in Brighton (similar projects now exist in Sheffield and the Wandsworth district of London). The concept links local authorities, parents, employers and voluntary organisations in a computer-run information bank. It acts as a resource base for everything to do with children, and aims to co-ordinate information in each community, thus building a country-wide network. The scheme makes itself accessible to parents by operating from high street shop-fronts, and includes more than childcare listings, embracing health and support services, places to visit, hire of equipment and much more. The Daycare Trust hopes this useful concept will soon spread.

Last-minute choices

It would certainly give peace of mind to know well in advance what your childcare arrangements will be. Sadly, with the patchy system that exists at present, few parents have this luxury – it seems that the only way to achieve it is to make an arrangement with a relative, who is usually happy to commit herself even before pregnancy begins.

If you decide to have a childminder, that is one thing – finding a good one who has a vacancy may be a totally different matter. Local authorities tell you to ring up about six to eight weeks before you are due to go back to work, as they cannot say in advance of this who might have a vacancy. Decisions then have to be taken after one or two visits to names on the list because there is so little time, and mothers are just grateful to find someone in their area. Given more time, they say they might be more choosy.

For many mothers, waiting until so late in the proceedings adds to the worry. They want to know who is going to care for their child well before going back to work. They want to visit and get to know this person and ease the child in gradually. The same is true of nurseries, where many mothers wait to hear whether or not there is a place for their child until pretty late in the day. The widely held belief that the best minders and nurseries are the least likely to have vacancies also adds to the tension.

In cases where the child is going to be left with a relative, plans are usually discussed when the decision to return to work is taken, sometimes even before the pregnancy. This gives the mother a sense of security. 'I'd never have become pregnant if I hadn't known my mum would look after the baby when I went back to work,' said one mother.

Who does the choosing?

In their study, *New Mothers at Work*, Peter Moss and Julia Brannen found that women divide fairly evenly between those – just over half – who feel that arranging the childcare is something that should be shared or done by whichever parent has the most time and opportunity, and those – just under half – who feel the job falls to the mother. Women in the latter group believe that searching for childcare is their job because it is 'their choice they are going back to work' and because 'you're the one who has to feel happy about leaving the baby'. In fact, the study found that arrangements *are* made mainly or wholly by mothers, with partners contributing discussion and occasionally visiting the nursery or childminder's house.

Your relationship with the carer

It helps to recognise that if the person who will care for your child really identifies with him, and grows to love him, there will inevitably be some natural jealousy between the two of you

– as indeed there often is between two caring parents. There are bound to be ways in which she does things differently from you, such as feeding or bathing your baby in a manner which irritates you. If she is basically doing a good job of caring for your baby, though, and supporting your relationship with him, then you will need to overcome these resentments and stirrings of jealousy.

There is a feeling expressed by mothers that while they are away at work the baby is giving his smiles, his first steps, his new skills, to the carer and mum is missing out. Pat Garrett describes how she returned from work one day and met the nanny leaving the house (her husband was with the baby). The nanny told Pat: 'There's a wonderful surprise waiting for you at home!' Her baby had taken her first step. At times like these, a mother can be overwhelmed by a sense of loss, as Pat described, feeling that she is losing out on the excitement of seeing her baby cross the hurdles of each thrilling stage of development.

Value the carer if she describes your baby's new tricks enthusiastically. If she does do things a little differently from you, it is not crucial. Babies are adaptable and can easily adjust to different handling – after all, they adjust to two parents and loving grandparents. But you do need to have a basis of trust, and a bedrock agreement for the relationship to work, and to know that on deeply held beliefs she follows your line.

If you have difficulties in your relationship with your carer, discuss with her your feelings of isolation and the 'tearing apart' that is necessary to concentrate on both work and mothering. Being frank may help to clear the air, and reveal ways in which the carer can help you build your relationship with your baby.

Do not be surprised, however, if some negative feelings are reciprocated. Your carer, too, may feel slightly possessive about 'her' baby and subconsciously resent you for leaving him, or think your childrearing ideas are off the mark. The hard truth is that most childminders choose this job in order to work and yet stay home with their own children. Deep down, your childminder or nanny may have a gut feeling that a mother should not leave her child, and this could create an unconscious aura of disapproval. If she steadily undermines you, however, or consistently makes you feel that you're inadequate, and only she knows it all – then you have the wrong person.

This last point is clearly a risk for a new mother up against an experienced carer. Some mothers in this situation abdicate all responsibility: 'She's doing a much better job than I could have done,' they say. Such a mother may withdraw into her work world, finding it increasingly difficult to handle the baby with confidence. Mothers need to learn to mother and a good carer will encourage this, not take over and exclude you.

Your baby's relationship with you

Strong personalities already, babies do have their own say, and often save up their important communications and emotions for mum. Holding on until she comes to collect him and then disintegrating is a common pattern. Trying to hold her attention possessively all evening and preventing her from getting supper or talking to someone else may be the toddler's way. If your child does this, see it as attachment to you!

Because a mother feels guilty at having left her baby to go to work, she may feel that his behaviour is her fault. A colicky baby who cries every evening, but not during the day with the carer, may simply be going through a phase in which this is his pattern. He might have done this whether or not his mother had left him, but she will respond anxiously and worriedly, blaming herself for this distress. Her tension is transferred to him and they can have a pretty traumatic reunion each evening. For a tired parent at the end of a working day, this can strain what little patience remains. She will feel disappointed that the time together she so looked forward to is transformed into this wretchedness.

Child development experts suggest that, in cases like these, you need to stand back and see the overall pattern of your child's development. Is it a stage? Can you change your response to it? Does it always stop by a certain time or in a particular way? Can your partner intervene to take away some of the tension the two of you are generating? Will a change in routine or feeding help?

Knowing common patterns babies go through, such as three-month colic, can help you to see it in perspective and to realise that – even had you stayed home – this baby would have gone through this stage. It also helps to know that coming through stressful times with your baby, and remaining calm, reinforces your relationship and confidence. The baby trusts you – after all you were the one who brought him through.

The trauma of parting

It is all too easy for a mother of a fussy baby to hand him over to a carer before getting through this early bonding phase, and therefore never gaining the intimate knowledge of the baby's needs or building trust. For this reason, there are paediatricians who recommend that you do not go back to work before at least four months after the birth in order to come through the tricky first three months and out the other side into the calm of the fourth month, cementing your bond and getting to know your child.

For those mothers who become very attached to their babies, parting may be especially painful. Dr Brazelton of Harvard Medical School identifies a serious problem when such a mother leaves her child in daycare. She may begin to withdraw from participation at the centre. She cares so much about leaving the baby, he argues, that the pain is too much to bear, and she suffers a form of grieving: 'She will feel guilty, inadequate, helpless, hopeless and even angry – "Why me?"' He goes on to describe three defences against these feelings of powerlessness and guilt in his book, *Working and Caring*:

Denial   Denying it matters either to you or the child

Projection   Projecting all good mothering on to the carer and taking all the bad for yourself, or vice versa; becoming unnecessarily jealous

Detachment   Pulling out to leave the baby in the other's care, not because you do not care but because it hurts so much to care

Brazelton explains it is not possible to get rid of these defences, but it is necessary to know they are there and likely to dominate your behaviour.

How the child is affected

At the vulnerable moment when they hand their child into the care of another, parents are anxious about the effect this will have on the child. Elizabeth Newsom, professor of developmental psychology at Nottingham University, has stressed the importance of continuity. The happiness and stability of children is critically affected by changes in the carer. 'Children under three find it quite difficult to cope in groups,' says Newsom. 'They need fairly stable relationships. It is important for the child to be able to identify one nursery nurse as his or hers.'

A crèche or nursery with a high staff turnover is possibly harmful for the child, as would be a constantly changing stream of nannies or *au pairs*. Studies show that, as long as care is consistent, dependable and of high quality, babies and toddlers develop equally well in maternal and non-maternal care. But how do you assess care and what do you look for?

Childminders

When choosing a childminder, there is a whole series of questions to which you will need answers. You may have to find out some of the information you need in a brief interview surrounded by kids; other aspects can only be gleaned by spending some time at the minder's house.

A checklist

Here is a checklist to get you started. You may have other questions of your own to add.

- What are the facilities (somewhere to play, somewhere to rest) and safety measures in the minder's house?
- Can the minder reach a nursery or library, playground or park?
- Can she drive (increasing her mobility and the facilities she can offer the children)?
- Does she take the children shopping with her?
- What is the routine of her day?
- What meals does she offer?
- How does she handle mealtimes?
- How would she cope in a crisis and what plans does she have for such an eventuality? Is there anyone she could call to be with some of the children if she were needed to rush one to a doctor?
- Does she smoke?
- What is the age range of her own children and the children she minds? Many people suggest that only one very young baby should be minded in a group of older children, some

of whom may attend a local nursery or even morning school. The age range is important: older children can help young ones but a small baby is quite difficult to fit into the routines of schoolchildren.

- How well does she cope with a group of children, and how sensitive is she to each one's needs? Are the other children happy, responsive, trusting? On leaving a baby with a carer, Kathy, an experienced childminder, has this to say: 'Someone looking after a small baby has to have endless patience for when they can't settle after feeds, etc, as I believe a baby senses tenseness and reacts to it . . . I would look for someone quite relaxed and happy to discuss how to look after *your* child, not someone who rushes to grab the child and cuddle, but who approaches the child sensibly, talking to the child occasionally to show she has noticed he or she's there, but not forcing herself on to the child.'

- Finally, how happy does the minder herself seem as a person? Eileen Gladwell, a childminder with 18 years' experience, considers that, in addition to finding a person who is intelligent and sensitive and who loves children, the minder should be reasonably happy herself – a point borne out by one mother's experience of a minder who lived in fear of an attack from her ex-husband.

Things to discuss with a minder

When you have finally chosen your minder, there are certain things you should discuss with her if you want things to run smoothly. To begin with, your child's health, allergies, skin problems, and so on, must all be made known to her. You should work out a procedure for emergencies and where you can be contacted, making certain the minder knows who your doctor is. Let your minder know whenever you are going to be late, or if fetching times are going to be erratic, so that neither she nor your child worries. Discuss toys, if you have a preference – one parent, for example, had to be a soldier in his homeland and did not want his child playing with a gun, until he saw him 'shooting' with his fingers – and lists of food that your child likes or does not like.

It is also very important to discuss discipline and values. If your minder shares your outlook on these, you may feel confident enough to leave decisions to her discretion; if you are at all unsure, however, you will need to spell out exactly what you want. Different parents handle these issues in different ways, as one childminder described: 'A good childminder has to be able to like other people's children enough to look after their every need, to treat them almost as her own, but defer to parents' wishes. A childminder cannot imprint her own values on another's child, only try to advise until the child has the chance to ask its own parents. One child has a dad who says I am in total control whilst he is at work; another child's parents have strict rules and tell me what I should do in a situation. You have to be a real diplomat to be a good childminder. You can always tell a good one as the minded children recommend her!'

Finally, remember that your child will have to learn to respect the minder's home and furniture and her children's toys – 'in some cases even if they don't respect their own'.

Communication

Communication between parents and minder is not always good. If a child has been ill over the weekend, for example, parents often fail to mention it: 'I get it from the child. They also don't say when they're going to be late.'

What seems to happen is that parents quickly relax after an initial period of settling in. They may then drop off the child in a rush and omit to say she has been picky with her food or restless, symptoms which could spell trouble and which the minder needs to know about, as Eileen says: 'I tell them when they fetch, if the child seems unwell something needs to be said. New parents tell me more; later on they think, "Oh, she'll be all right, Eileen will cope." '

Social life

You may be concerned that because your child is cared for by a minder, she is missing out on the social life generated at the school gate. When collecting their children, non-working parents socialise with each other and do not include the children who are collected by the minder. 'Parents don't chat to you or invite you, they don't talk to me if they know I'm the minder,' is the experience of one minder. On the other hand, your child will have the company of the other children at the minder's, together forming a family group.

Parting

The first partings are always difficult, as one childminder describes: 'Mums go off in tears: "Am I doing the right thing?" [they ask]. Parents of small babies worry that the baby can't tell you about her day. Equally for me, it's hard to part with a child who leaves me. I find if I know a child is leaving, I withdraw gradually from him.'

If possible, give yourself plenty of time to settle your child and ease her in gradually. Stay with her initially, for several days if necessary. When you first leave her, come back after a short while to reassure her you will return.

Minders, nursery staff and nannies all agree that a child who is in tears when her mother leaves may recover quickly when she is out of sight and be fine. Many mums admit to sneaking back and peering through windows unseen or listening at the door to hear if the sobbing has died away – frequently to find that the child has settled in the meantime.

Feeling positive about the step you are taking will transfer itself to your child. If you are very tense, she may feel the same and come to believe that there is something to be feared in parting.

Difficulties

One of the difficulties in using a childminder comes at that tricky moment when parents come to collect their children. The qualities needed to operate at the workplace are very different from the nurturing, intuitive qualities needed for childcare. Mothers report that having to switch rapidly from one rôle to the other causes problems, especially when they are very tired at the end of the day. It is a matter of tuning in again.

Helen, a single parent, describes the moment of changeover after a full day at the office: 'I find having to go and pick up C from the childminder – that's when the big crunch happens for me. I'm going to collect her and I have to listen to the childminder telling me all this when I just want to rush through the door with her and bring her home. It's about 20 minutes and I'm like this . . . [wrung out]. The stress of this is the lowest part of the day. It can be grim and that's when I do the real switch-over from thinking on the train, as I sit there, what I'm going to do and what's got to be done the next day at the office.'

Another, more serious problem has to do with the personal qualities of the minder herself. Childminders *do* vary tremendously, ranging from ghastly to the gold-dust variety – there is the kind who sits the kids in front of the television all day, and the kind who offers books, crayons and cuddles. Parents frequently choose to overlook what they perceive as shortcomings, either because they are grateful for the overall quality of the care, or because they are so dependent on it they dare not admit their fears.

Picture the scene: the unhappy mother, rushed off her feet, hands over her child on the doorstep apologising because she is off to work again and may be late back. The minder prises a wailing child from her. Grateful to have someone with whom to leave Danny, our mum swallows her anxieties about junk food and outdoor activity for fear of alienating the carer. She tells herself the carer knows what she is doing and hurries off.

Discussing a childminder with one mother, I asked, 'Is she perceptive?'

'Not awfully, I don't think,' came the reply, 'but she's a very good child rearer; she's brought up five children and that's the only level on which I can communicate with her. I find it sometimes very trying. I can't relate to her in any other way. I used to worry that I was depriving my daughter of intellectual stimulus. The thing that most upset me when I first left her there was this enormous television in the corner of the room which was on all day, and that really alarmed me. I'd never come across this before, and I'm so used to it now I don't even notice it. She doesn't either. Yes, it really worries me, the TV.'

This mother feels that the childminder is far more experienced than she is herself, and is using this to justify leaving her child with her – despite worries about lack of intelligent conversation and the constant barrage of the telly. In order to justify to herself her act of leaving her child in this situation, she repeatedly told me what a good 'child rearer' the minder was. The term had an almost agricultural ring to it, as if the child was being 'reared', like a puppy. Meanwhile, however, her mental stimulation was being neglected. High-quality community childcare, with a national programme for children's development, would remove this problem.

Parents also spoke of being more indulgent with their children in the short evening hours they had together, or the rushed weekends, than the carer might be. To banish any ideas of implied criticism, however, they then rushed to the minder's defence, saying what a wonderful job she was doing – much better, in fact, than they could do themselves. This seemed to be a way of redressing any guilt they might feel about leaving their child with a minder in the first place.

On the subject of indulgence, I also asked, 'Do you think she plays you up against the childminder or vice versa?' Frequently I heard the same answer: 'Oh, she knows I'm much softer, and she gets away with things she can't with Lorna. There are times on a Monday evening when I pick her up when the minder says, "You spoiled her this weekend. I have had a very hard day with her today." She can always see the change in her on a Monday. I'm very lucky in my childminder, and I think she, so far, has brought my daughter up better than I could have done.'

This pattern, arising out of underlying guilt and dependence on the minder, reinforces a first-time mother's insecurity. As time passes and habits are set, she feels increasingly less able to discuss concerns with the minder and to tell her that she would like her to do things *her* way. This kind of situation highlights the importance of getting problems out in the open as soon as they rear their head – the longer you leave it, the harder it gets.

Daycare

From autumn 1990 UK parents can look for a kite mark standard of quality which is being prepared to cover group care of children under five. Institutions will be inspected annually.

Buildings and equipment

Site, buildings and equipment are the first things that parents notice when they make their initial visit to a day nursery. Parents often feel very cheered when they see a light and airy building and a playground with trees, especially if they live in a flat themselves. But buildings, though important, are not everything. Here are some points to look out for on your first visit:

- Is there outside space and, if not, are the children taken to a park or playground? What is the route and how safe is it?
- How often do the children go outside and are they supervised?
- What is the condition of the play equipment in the playground?

Shiny, new equipment is less important than space to run about in and boxes and blankets with which to make dens. Equipment in bad repair, however, could be positively dangerous.

- Are toys in good condition and safe?
- How safe is the building itself? Could a child fall out of the window? Are there any uncovered electric sockets, or medicines or detergents within reach? (On registering, the nursery will have been checked against the fire regulations and the amount of space per child.)

Resources

As well as checking out the condition of equipment and toys, have a look at quality and availability of the resources:

- Is there a good supply of interesting toys, books and equipment, crayons, paints and puzzles? Are they accessible to the children, or stored in a cupboard and seldom used?
- Is there an opportunity for music, singing and dancing, or for playing the piano or other musical instruments?
- Are the children encouraged to use the resources freely?
- Are the materials anti-sexist and anti-racist? Many campaigners for good practice in nurseries have drawn attention to this issue. Does this matter to you?

Policies

To find out what the nursery's policies are, observe the staff in action and ask specific questions:

- Do you agree with their policies on discipline, education and integration of children with special needs, or babies with older children (termed family grouping)?
- Is there a commitment to equal opportunities for staff, parents and all children?
- Are the children encouraged to be considerate of one another? What happens when someone is bullied? Are children comforted quickly when necessary? How do staff handle an obviously unhappy child?
- What is the nursery's approach to settling in new children?
- What is the procedure if a child takes ill during the day?
- Will the nursery keep you informed about your child?

- What do children do in a typical day? Are projects imaginative and stimulating? Is there provision for simple science and mathematics – wet and dry sand play, opportunities to discover what floats and what sinks, along wth measuring and pouring activities?

General atmosphere

The general 'feel' of the nursery will also give you clues as to whether this is the right place for your child:

- How do the children react to strangers? Are they relaxed and friendly?
- Are they busy and active with enough equipment for all?
- Are there story-telling and chatting times when the staff encourage children to talk or listen? Do the staff engage children in conversations?
- What is the ratio of staff to children? This is laid down by the local authority but may not be kept to at all times. One adult to five children aged two to five years is suggested, and one adult to three babies. What is the staff's attitude to parent involvement? Are parents always welcome?

Staff

The staff – as individals with their own special qualities and approach – are the most important resource of a nursery; a wonderful staff can make up a great deal for any lack of material provision. I have seen nurseries without much in the way of expensive equipment where imaginative staff used simple, waste materials to create art projects worthy of gallery space, and where warmth, affection and humour enlivened the pokiest room. Find opportunities for chats with staff well before starting at the nursery:

- Do you actually like the staff? Your child will receive unspoken messages from your response to them.
- How do they receive you? Are they willing to show you around, and talk about the policies of the nursery, and your child's particular habits and likes? Do they pay attention to you when you arrive in the evening, giving and receiving information, or are they in a hurry to see you go? Do they help to ease the pain of separation?

- What is their training and experience? Do they understand children's developmental stages?
- Is the head teacher or person in charge good with people, and able to handle staff and children well?
- Do the staff help children transfer from one activity to another in a sensitive and caring manner? Do they attempt to draw in a child who seems left out? Do they respect the child as an individual – his rhythm, his need for quiet time, fantasy or cuddles?
- How do they handle mealtimes and toilet accidents?
- What is the staff turnover like? Frequent changes will upset your child's stability.
- Will you feel your child is in good hands?

Nannies

'There is nothing like gut instinct to go by,' says Pat. 'Oh, it's the voice. I could tell at once on the phone . . .' says Eve.

These women are describing that something extra that makes you take to someone, an empathy at first sight. 'You can have people who, on paper, look as though they've done the lot, but if you don't actually take to them as people . . .' Pat voices an important issue. Your child will take to the nanny so much more easily if he senses that you like her and respond easily to her.

Apart from simply liking a prospective nanny as a person, there are still important hurdles to clear, both before and after you employ her.

Begin as you mean to go on

All the qualities that are listed under *Childminders* (see page 105) apply to nannies, but getting on with your nanny is even more vital because she will be in your own home, perhaps even living in. The ideal is a smooth working relationship that leads to friendship, and offers love and security to the children. All too often, though, there are tales of expectations dashed, or conversely of exploitation, resulting in a power struggle and breakdown of the relationship.

Balancing the employer/employee relationship is vital from the start, and personal and working boundaries should be agreed as early as possible – it is too late to say anything later, mothers tell me. Parents who are otherwise effective and assertive may find themselves meekly deferring to a nanny who becomes more and more powerful in the household. If a problem arises and the nanny threatens to walk out, the parents will do everything they can to accommodate her demands. 'She knows she has us over a barrel,' says Sue. 'I felt she always had the upper hand; so I turned a blind eye to her sulkiness because I depended on her.' 'I do feel I have to bend over backwards to keep her. I'm scared to say anything in case she leaves. Our whole household and two jobs depend on her,' says Valerie.

But mothers learn fast – when starting with a new nanny a mother will say all that was left unsaid during the stay of the last one.

Checking up

Parents recommend that you check the nanny's references and do not deceive yourself into ignoring them. An agency will provide some background material, but it is essential to ring up previous employers yourself.

Mothers have also told me how essential it is to pop home unexpectedly, or have a friend or relative drop in for you. Nannies have been discovered watching adult videos, while six-year-olds play on their own nearby. One particularly shocking story involved a girl who abused a child when he refused to eat. She salted his food very heavily and forced him to eat it. Another time she was seen to push a knife down his throat.

These horror stories are the exception rather than the rule, and there are many happy tales of nannies who are gems, and whom the children adore and visit for years to come. But it pays to be warned.

Common problems

One fairly common problem is the nanny who wants to spend time with her boyfriend. She arranges to meet him at a café and your child spends the morning strapped into the pushchair while she chats up her friend. This can become a regular event.

She may also have her boyfriend come to stay, or go out late too many nights a week, so that she is too exhausted during the day to do her job properly.

Clearing the status of boyfriends is a sticky problem best deal with before he is on the scene. Nannies can abuse your trust by ringing intercontinental friends on your phone.

Use of the car is another potential minefield. Even when a girl has a licence, some parents are not happy with her driving. 'She had no real road sense,' explains one. There are cases of Nanny driving a car without a licence and with the baby on the floor. Merely accepting that she is a licensed driver is not enough, it seems. You need to go out in the car with her often and check how she handles the car before allowing her to drive the children. Safety procedures, seat belts, car seats, and child-proof locks on doors all need to be checked regularly.

Social life

Parents often find that the nanny seeks out other nannies for companionship and your children are thrown together with other charges. These may not be the children you or your kids would choose as friends. The nanny may, in fact, neglect your child's existing friends, while their mothers may not choose to sit and have coffee with the nanny in your place. Groups of nannies or *au pairs* absorbedly chatting, as the children run wild, are a common sight in parks. The opposite of this is a lonely, isolated nanny who seldom goes out and becomes morose. This is a delicate area in which you need to strike a balance. A happy girl is vital and all adults caring for small children need other adult company.

Nannies' rights

Just as you expect the nanny to respect your boundaries, so you should respect hers. Parents can exploit the nanny, allowing children to call her on her day off, expecting her to get up to all night-time cries, and coming in later than arranged again and again.

Live-in nannies complain of no allowance for a private life, and no consideration if they are ill: 'The attitude just tends to be, well, take an aspirin, you'll be all right, just lie on the sofa and the children can play.' Nannies also say that, on falling ill, some parents expect nanny to care for them as well as keep the children quiet and out of the way.

One of the most common irritations is being asked where any missing item has got to. 'I'm expected to know where his glasses are or her garlic squeezer,' said one nanny. 'It's as if they're suggesting I've hidden or taken it.' Then there are the fathers who walk around semi-nude or make suggestive jokes.

A nanny sees herself as a professional and asks to be treated as such. The difficulty is to maintain an employer/employee relationship in a situation of such intense intimacy. Careful interviewing, if possible meeting the girl's family, checking references and carefully outlining the job are the first steps in getting this relationship going.

13

Workplace nurseries

'The ramifications for the family are quite scary,' said a single working mother whose child attends a workplace nursery. 'It's a disadvantage in negotiation.'

As perks go, the privilege, now tax deductible, of a precious place in one of the few new workplace nurseries has been compared with that of having a company car. In fact, it has more in common with the tied cottage of yesteryear. Workplace nurseries are not the answer.

Cost as criterion

The government encourages employers to tackle the critical problem of childcare in the UK, which has one of the lowest childcare provisions in the EC. The massive costs of this provision are being shunted on to the shoulders of employers who will need to recruit and keep trained staff in a period of predicted shortage after the recession. This is a response to the shortage of workers, not a positive response to the needs of the child.

Setting up a workplace nursery is not cheap. According to the National Childminding Association, it can cost up to £500,000 in the first year to set up and run a crêche for 75 children, and ongoing costs start at £290,000. Suitable space is hard to find in valuable business premises in industrial or commercial areas (the rare purpose-built crêches out of town clearly have an advantage here).

Faced with the figures, employers will naturally only look at the problem from a commercial point of view. Kristine Coppersmith, of the Cambridge Childcare Consultancy, says, 'Companies want the bottom line. Cash is their overriding interest, but quality where childcare is concerned cannot be compromised. If I'm too expensive they go elsewhere and get lower quality – it's putting children into the marketplace.' This is a very different approach from one in which a nation values its children and sees them as the promise of the future, and therefore attends to their welfare and educational needs with one goal – that of providing what is best for the child.

We have got it all wrong if childcare provision is allowed to fall into the commercial sector, to be dealt with according to commercial criteria. Nursery franchises are due to be set up, providing staff in identical uniforms and set menus; soon we'll hear talk of rental rates per square foot of child.

Consultants have appeared, advertising 'a blueprint for conducting the business of childcare' which will 'produce well-balanced and alert children', as though human beings were a product on a conveyor belt to be manufactured in a 'bespoke nursery'. There is no regulatory system for monitoring or registering such 'consultants'. 'Ill-informed people are opening up consultancies where standards of quality and good practice are not on their brief – only square feet per child and number of workers required. Women have to shoulder a lot of this blame,' says Kristine, 'because they are desperate and will accept almost any care.'

Parental dependence

Dependence on a workplace nursery puts employees in a weak position. When it comes to negotiating with workers, employers will have the advantage that a worker with a child happily settled in the nursery can hardly say 'no' to new conditions of service for fear of losing her job. It also makes it harder to make career moves. 'If we presuppose a workplace nursery of good quality and good practice, what does a woman do offered a better job elsewhere, where the nursery may be of lesser quality?' asks Kristine Coppersmith.

The following two examples illustrate the difficulties. One single mother of a two-year-old has entered a freelance agreement with a company, call them Company A. She has taken up a place in their newly opened workplace nursery. Her child is well settled. She has taken advantage of the freedom gained and set up her own business and is able to expand the service she offers Company A. In addition she values the assistance with her son Mike, after looking after him alone. 'He gains enrichment and the broadening of his social life,' she says. Now Company A want her to sign an exclusive agreement. Bang goes her hard-won new business if she does; bang goes her stable childcare and freedom to work if she does not.

Marina, wanting a second child, knows that, if she takes maternity leave now, her two-year-old son will lose his place in the company crêche, and she has little chance of finding him a place near home. He would lose friends and stimulus at a moment when jealousy of the new baby might be a problem. Does she wait until he starts school to have her next child?

Both women would have been infinitely better off with good local provision offering reasonable hours. They are much wiser now than when they 'eagerly and naively accepted that first offer of a place'.

Some women describe the existence of the company crêche as a subtle pressure on them to return to work earlier than they might otherwise have done, and describe the crêche as 'a mixed blessing'.

Mike's mum has the last word: 'I've become aware of huge political and financial pressures to make workplace nurseries seem to be a success, and I fear that overeagerness to allow women more freedom of choice in what, where and when they work is a minefield.'

Questions to be asked

There are other grey areas in the realm of workplace nurseries, and light needs to be thrown upon them.

* **How secure are workplace nurseries?**

  'How long-term are these nurseries? What if there is a new policy in the company, or a change of decision maker?' asks Kristine Coppersmith. At any point the crêche may become 'uncommercial to run', or workers may be replaced by technology and the unit closed down. And if employers are serious about maintaining a nursery, how serious are they about the standard of care, and how suited is it to the children who attend? Is the level of care that of a crêche, a playgroup, or a nursery school?

* **Who gets a place?**

  How do you decide who gets the places in your workplace

crêche? If male employees avail themselves of a staff facility, this might free their wives to go and work for the company's competitor. How, in allocating places, do you measure the need of one employee over another, or your company's need for this particular worker's services? Already there are stories of in-fighting and jockeying for places. Will it really be first come, first served, as the Midland Bank say their scheme will be? What if a key person high up in the bank should suddenly need a place?

How will quality be monitored and maintained?

Will it be maintained in the face of cost-cutting drives? 'The government urges employers to set up nurseries, but provides no funds for infrastructure,' says Penny Craig of Workplace Nurseries Limited. 'Under-fives' officers are concerned about quality and standards, but without sufficient resources from local government, there is very little they can do.' Once a nursery is registered and has complied with initial requirements, there is little quality and good practice control. 'Childcare in this country is piecemeal; there is no comprehensive strategy,' says Penny.

Angela Phillips, author of *Until They Are Five*, points out that the rôle of local authorities here is 'punitive not supportive, they can close down an unregistered nursery,' but 'in Australia and New Zealand, the local authority can give money to the voluntary sector to put premises in order'.

A better way

Why does the UK not learn from the failed experiments in other European countries? 'We're so far behind in type and level of provision,' says Penny Craig. 'This may be due to a peculiarly British view that it is a private matter to sort out, whereas the European view is that under-fives provision benefits parents, children and industry.'

Workplace nurseries alone are not the answer. 'In France,' explains Mary Michaels of the National Childcare Campaign, 'it is generally thought better for the child to be cared for in the locality' – and they have had 30 years of experience. It has been found that the best model is community-based childcare, functioning as a partnership between local authority, employers and parents.

This view is supported by the National Childcare Campaign, who want parents to have a range of options, a 'choice of service for parents with childcare to accommodate their various needs to work, study or participate in other activities outside the home'. The Campaign wants more emphasis on children's needs and involvement of local people and parents in the management of projects. They advocate 'equal opportunity for all children in quality daycare projects that are anti-racist and non-sexist'. At the moment this seems a far-off dream.

Twelve-point plan for effective childcare

- Get as much information on childcare as you can, as early as possible.
- Recognise your child's behaviour patterns – disintegrating at home time, or possessiveness – as signs of attachment to you.
- See phases objectively, and do not blame yourself too readily.
- Experiment with routine to suit you and your baby.
- Remember that coming through a stressful time and remaining in control reinforces your relationship with your baby.
- Try to gain an intimate knowledge of your baby's needs.
- Aim for stability and continuity of care.
- Do not let a carer undermine your confidence.
- Do not let jealousy harm your relationship with the carer.
- Watch that you do not withdraw into your work world because it hurts so much to care.
- Do not deny your feelings in parting, and recognise your baby's feelings, too.
- Do not project all good mothering on to the carer, taking all the bad for yourself (or vice versa).

How do you recognise a depressed baby?

So you have found a place for your baby and now you are worrying about how good the care is when you are away at work. If only the baby could tell you about her day. Well, she can, through unspoken signals and behaviour, alert you to whether or not something is wrong.

Babies do show signs of depression which could be warning signs. These have been documented in those studies of babies in institutions made in the early 1950s. Lack of 'mother love' and stimulation, it was shown, caused failure to thrive. It is unlikely to happen today when childcare practice has been so strongly influenced by these studies, and media and childcare manuals have publicised the concept that love and communication are essential for babies. But it is possible that a baby in a nursery with too little adult-child interaction, lying for hours in a cot and only fed and changed routinely, may begin to show some depression. It is also possible if she is left with a carer who is herself depressed.

Maternal deprivation

Since John Bowlby's work became so widely accepted it has been universally believed that young children need their mothers or a constant mother substitute more than anything else. (It is partly thanks to these studies that mothers are now encouraged to stay with their young children in hospitals.) Bowlby argued that if babies have no opportunity to become attached to a mother figure, they become adults who lack a conscience, and are unable to give or receive affection. They cannot form close relationships.

He also noticed that where a child has become attached to the mother, a separation in infancy can cause permanent disturbance (he was talking here of total separation, of course, not simply a matter of a few hours). He found that if separation is prolonged the child becomes withdrawn, even if the mother and child are reunited later.

These findings have led to a pervasive belief that it is harmful for mothers to go out to work, leaving young children. The guilt and anguish many mothers suffer on account of this is reinforced by the popularly held view that they are somehow 'abandoning their children'.

A reassessment

In *Maternal Deprivation Reassessed*, Michael Rutter and others have criticised some of Bowlby's findings. They were done in bleak post-war institutions. They did not reflect children who lived at home with loving parents, and who were cared for warmly during working hours. The conditions in which these test babies were kept amounted to near solitary confinement. They were deprived of stimulus and social contact. It was this combination of all the circumstances, rather than only the lack of a mother, which caused such intellectual backwardness in the institutional children studied.

Rutter argues that the important point is for the child to be attached to one *constant* figure, and this need not automatically be the mother. Bowlby himself later changed his stance, saying that more than one supporting figure in the child's life was acceptable.

The reason for giving you all this background is plain. When you are tackled by some do-gooder who says you are irreparably harming your child, you will understand the origin of this thinking. You can turn to page 59 and read about studies which show that children do well in care. Meanwhile it pays to watch your child carefully.

Signs of depression

A baby who is showing signs of depression may grow quieter and quieter. She may appear overwhelmed by your greeting, or by normal family noises such as those made by other children. She will not respond when you try to play with her, and may avert her eyes. She may look pale and lose her appetite; some babies continue feeding fairly normally but lose weight despite this. Watch out for drastic personality changes, and an avoidance of personal contact, a sort of withdrawing from the world around her (a healthy baby will search for personal contact and seek attention). If coupled with weight loss, a baby may be categorised as 'failing to thrive'.

Symptoms such as these may alert you to the fact that your baby's daycare is not caring enough: she may not be getting individual attention, or the general hubbub of the nursery may be overwhelming her. She needs some one-to-one attention. If the situation continues, the baby will no longer expect or seek the attention she needs in order to thrive. She will not only lose weight, but her immune system may also be affected.

These symptoms can, of course, also mean that the child is simply ill. But if they persist over a couple of weeks, you should seriously consider the care you have chosen.

Warning signs in older children

Many families laughingly joke that Mum has 'eyes in the back of her head', that she always knows what is going on, even if the kids try to hide something from her. A joke this may be, but in fact the mother/child relationship depends on the mother's being very observant and responsive. Every mother needs to develop this gift, regardless of whether she goes out to paid work or not. Danielle, a child psychoanalyst, explains: 'If the mother isn't noticing all the tiny signs, and many are less obvious than these, then this is something to do with the mothering. I don't think you can attribute that to the mother being at work.'

Picking up warning signals is essential. To do this well you need to be aware of your child's habits and personality, all the special little quirks that make him such a unique individual. When he is under stress, you may notice any one of these or several: a big falling off at school, bedwetting, withdrawal and aggression. He may reject you or be 'difficult to reach'. There may be disturbed sleep at night, babyish behaviour, regression and hanging on to old habits – your child reasons that, if he is still a baby, Mum will stay home with him. All these are signals that something is troubling him.

Your child needs to know, and be shown, that he is important to you, even when you are not with him, and there are a number of ways you can do this:

- Try phoning your child during the day for a chat.
- Leave something of yours with him to keep for you until you return: this will make him feel valued and useful.
- Take something he has made, like a drawing, with you to work.
- Show your child your place of work; this is especially useful if he sees you have a photo of him or his drawing up on your desk; then he will know you think of him during your absences.
- Bring home stamps for a collection, or other small items that show you have been thinking of your child during the week.
- If you have to be away for a couple of days or longer, you can write letters or postcards, or do drawings, and post them before leaving to make certain they arrive on the day of departure. My daughter once had a favourite book about Ralph the Rhino who stayed at the Ritz; I sent her a letter on Ritz-headed paper, saying I had called in there and had seen greedy gourmet Ralph, and he had asked about her.
- Read bedtime stories on to tape, and they can be played back in your absence bringing the comforting sound of your voice.

If your care situation is good, such small tokens of your love and interest can do nothing but help and add to the benefit your child is receiving; they cannot, however, make up for bad care. If you do notice any adverse signs in an older child, do look carefully into your care arrangements. Perhaps your child is not getting enough personal nurturing, or he may be having problems at school. This is his way of sending a cry for help.

Part Five

Life choices

•

'There was a script for wife and there was a script for
mother; and then there was another script that I was
writing on the sidelines – you always wrote it dark corners,
and that was the script of a woman working outside the
home. I lived three lives and they weren't integrated.'
Carmel Niland, Australian campaigner for women's rights,
in Susan Mitchell, *Tall Poppies Too* (1991). First woman
President of the Anti-Discrimination Board, and first
Women's Adviser in New South Wales.

15

Quality of life

'The thing is that work ought to be enjoyable just because it's work. You should discipline yourself to enjoy what you do. Even if it's peeling potatoes. When you're writing a novel, typing those million or however many words you do from the first draft to the last, it's tiring! There's a lot of shit work. What turns you on is the sheer satisfaction of having created something out of nothing, then polishing it till it shines.'

Colleen McCullough in *Tall Poppies Too*
by Susan Mitchell (1991)

As people talked about their frantic timetables, their harassed efforts to cope, and the stresses and strains of the dual-career lifestyle, I felt I had to ask about the quality of their own lives. There had to be more to it than the treadmill.

So many described the nightmare of the early-morning rush, dressing the baby in her cot while still asleep, rushing the kids through their Coco-pops and dropping them off at school and minder before racing to be at work on time, giving their all through the day and coming home exhausted to face tired, crochety kids and howling baby, with all the neglected housework looming. But what about personal time and space, I asked. Was there ever time for adult contact with partner or friends, time for you alone? Did the family share and enjoy time together and how? And what did *you* do for your own enrichment and relaxation – or just for plain *fun*?

Improving the quality of life

There were very different interpretations of what was meant by quality of life – and the ways to achieve it. An amazing number of people mentioned music in one form or another, from listening to their son's heavy metal group to classical purity. Sport, hobbies and just being alone doing nothing were all suggested. Some lucky couples manage the occasional lunch together. Sunday walks in the countryside or sailing offered precious privacy.

Elizabeth, who works in a hospice for the terminally ill and is a follower of yoga, believes that quality of life has to do with your general approach to life as a whole. In order to have this quality, you need to encompass birth and death, she says: 'It's important for a family unit how we're born and it's equally important how we die.' Elizabeth gave birth to her son at home and believes that the 'type of delivery you have is important, it's like falling in love a bit,' and that this determines the relationship with the child.

Being able to offer her son the quality of life she wants for him means that Elizabeth works night duty 'so that if Michael is ill or it is school holidays, I am there. I can take him to school and be at school events. The compromise is you don't get promotion and the day people get more satisfaction as they see the doctors and the social workers.'

Yoga has been a tremendous resource for Elizabeth. 'I started yoga before I married, you need some inner resource. Some weeks, like last week, we have 14 deaths, of which five were young. I go swimming, too. It's sometimes hard to sleep. I try not to worry about that, I don't really think death is that terrible, I'm very positive. Yoga offered a peaceful way to cope. I don't get very much money, but I've balanced it out.'

Those little extras

For Elizabeth, quality of life definitely does not depend on having money, but for others it was precisely the additional money brought in by the mother's work that made all the difference. Pauline, for example, feels that working is worth it because her earnings pay for the special extras for her children. 'The things that make the difference,' she says. Both her daughters are musical. Pauline, who was previously an ambulance driver, works evenings stacking supermarket shelves from 8 pm to 12 pm or 9 pm to 1 am to pay for music lessons which, she is convinced, will add to her children's quality of life, not only now but when they are adults. She herself paints on silk for a hobby.

Judi, too, feels that her earnings make all the difference to the quality of life of her family, but in more major ways: 'From the basics upwards. We wouldn't be able to live in the house we live in and wouldn't be able to have the holidays and the super activities we do together without my working.'

Job satisfaction

Not everyone, however, looked to time outside of work for what they defined as quality of life. Some found their satisfaction in the work itself: 'My work is who I am,' says Anita, who has a job in advertising, while others added: 'My work isn't just a profession, it's part of my identity . . . it's such an important part of my sense of self I express through my work,' 'I enjoy the responsibility and rewards of working full time. This year I acquired a directorship and share-holding in the company after four years' hard work,' and 'Our marriage is stronger and happier for my going out to work. The children see more of their father than they ever did before.'

Polly Toynbee explains that the excitement and pace of life at work is different from what happens at home. There is an addictive adrenalin flow that comes with the pressure, the big decisions and the high-powered meetings. 'In the news, we're rushing for breakfast, one o'clock, six and nine. It's great fun, it's terrifically exciting and fuels the adrenalin. The people I work with are an extraordinarily enjoyable, clever, interesting, cheerful lot. So all of it on a day-to-day basis is great fun. You're always on the edge of a precipice, you could certainly make a catastrophic error. You're living at this high-pitched level of excitement, it becomes a kind of addictive form of life in itself.'

Being, not doing

For a large number of people, quality of life meant time with the family – time definitely not spent on chores or banal tasks, but simply on enjoying being together.

Kirsten takes a simple route to relaxation and family time: 'We have a dog and take him for walks in the surrounding fields and woods. We need that bit of peace, even if it is a rainy day. You feel refreshed afterwards. On Sundays, we might all go down to the meadows for a walk. My husband swims and does TM [transcendental meditation]. I play the piano and go to church. It is very necessary to have time with the children and be able to do things you can share and to build up a feeling of togetherness. It is easy to let things slip, and the children slide away for no particular reason.'

Deborah Owen, a literary agent, also praises the benefits of simple, rural activities, of just enjoying nature. Talking of family weekends in the country, she says how much she enjoys leaving one territory for another 'which has a totally different atmosphere without the pressures. I'm sure that's what keeps us together. It is very romantic there. Much as we love London . . . the phone rings . . . I think being interested in something together, the husband and the wife, is first of all important. I've never loved sailing as much as David . . . but I like the togetherness of it. Talking in the boat, you learn to respect the elements, you talk about nature, understanding that it's still a force to be reckoned with.'

Cindy Chant stresses how important it is to spend time together peacefully at home, not actually doing anything in particular: 'I pot a few plants, my daughter is revising nearby.' She deplores households where the parents' idea of giving to their children takes the form of everything money can buy, and says that, in her rounds as a health visitor, she comes across children who have every material comfort but are emotionally deprived.

Danielle echoes this view. She works as a psychoanalyst with children, which is often extremely stressful. She is home with her son on several afternoons after school: 'I reckon that I am absent the maximum that is tolerable to me, and what is tolerable to me defines what is tolerable to him.' She emphasises how vital it is to be companionably peaceful at home for a child, and for him to learn to amuse himself. 'Learn to be together, peacefully, not doing something every second. Spend easy relaxed time together doing your own thing. Respect each other as people with your own identity. We have an idea that children must be organised and "busy" all the time, thus denying them time just to be.'

Elizabeth Hughes, a hospice nurse, believes quality is a less tangible element than material goods or comforts. She, too, is against children rushing around on a constant prearranged timetable: 'Children need peace to dream or to play the piano. To come home is restful – they can't be rushing about from carer to carer.'

Something has to go

Hobbies are certainly one of the first things to go for women who work full time. Deborah Owen is no exception: 'It almost goes without saying in my generation that if you work, that means that the sewing circle or singing evening went – forget it, frankly

I mean your hobby is considered your work and you chose that which, after all, takes a huge chunk of the day, and you devote the rest of your time to your family.'

Now working hectic hours at the BBC, Polly Toynbee has previously done other work that made fewer demands on her time, such as feature writing. But now she says, 'In my present job, I feel there is almost no cultural input. I'm not even inputting for my work in the sense of reading what I need to, having lunches with people, meeting people, having contact. It's all produce, produce, produce. I no longer can go to the theatre, never go to movies, occasionally watch a bit of TV. That part of my life is completely seized up. We see friends a bit, but not in the kind of relaxed way I used to – not like having lunch with an old friend. I hardly have any time to read. It's a major loss and eventually it will make me a lesser person.'

Polly used to work at a very different pace while bringing up her daughters and now has one of them and a much younger little son at home. She says this new way of life is 'a new phenomenon for me. It's strange to come at it in your forties, rather than the other way round. It told me an awful lot I didn't know about men and the way men work and how they balance their work and home. I realise that I live like a man in a way that I never have, and I realise that I'm going to atrophy like a man if I'm not careful.'

In times of stress, what also deteriorates is the quality of the time spent together. 'What gives, I think, is relaxed time with Adam. Things become very functional – have a bath, have a meal – and just lolling around and relaxing is gone,' says Danielle. 'By the end of term, we're all crawling around trying to survive.'

At times like these, inner resources dwindle and a sense of humour is an early casualty, say several women. Many mothers, close to a knife edge, explode irrationally when a child does something they would normally tolerate or even laugh at. A mother might then also be less in tune with a child. Empathy, so vital between parent and child, is lessened with stress.

Fitting it all in

There are families in which a regular pattern helps produce successful 'together time'. In Vivienne's family, for example, meals taken together and religious activities form a structure. Vivienne is a solicitor and her husband a specialist physician with a busy practice. She told me that they 'do relaxing activities together, we laugh a lot together, we usually have a family supper, so we do a lot of talking and we have a religious affiliation. I take them to movies and plays, they go camping with their father in the mountains, sometimes one at a time.'

But there are dangers if your routine becomes too rigid. Remember single mother Miriam in Barbara Kingsolver's story, *Quality Time*, who believed organisation was her religion: 'Miriam could no more abandon her orderly plan than a priest would swig down the transubstantiated wine and toss out wafers like Frisbees over the heads of those waiting to be blessed . . . Miriam's motto is that life is way too complicated to leave to chance.' She and her five-year-old daughter live life on a tight schedule, without two minutes to spare: 'Their dance card, so to speak, is filled.'

In their attempts to control everything and have it all run like clockwork, the Miriams of this world may become oblivious to the needs and potential of the moment. On listening to so many people talk about being very organised and making schedules and lists for everything, I felt that they were leaving no space for the unexpected – it would throw them right off track. One lost button or burst tyre could bring the whole house down like dominoes. There is also a loss of spontaneity. What if it's a beautiful day on Saturday – would you simply drop everything and go out to the park? Not if you run life to a rigid schedule.

Nor can rigid schedules cope with those unsuitable moments when your child pins you down to discuss major money matters, or to ask 'Can we have a dog?' or even 'Should I go on the Pill?' Some mothers find the nuts-and-bolts conversations the hardest – the ones about detailed arrangements and pocket money arrears and IOUs – whereas 'having wonderful conversations about the more intangible things, feelings, or relationships, I adore that, I can be drawn out of any mood to have conversations like that,' said Deborah Owen.

The problems of over-scheduling are beautifully illustrated in Penelope Lively's short story, *In Olden Times*. In the story, the busy mother apportions time and money in her head constantly: 'She lived by the clock. Her days were apportioned, hour by hour, parcelled up into time at work, time for sleeping, time for house-cleaning, for shopping, time for children. An hour, a half hour, 10 minutes. Time for love-making; time for ironing, for cooking, for taking a bath. A crisis meant time borrowed from one sector and forever owed – the entire week flung out of order by an emergency visit to the surgery or a faulty washing machine or car that would not start. And each day was punctuated by the rigorous, inescapable blasts of the whistle.' As she rushes through her timetable, this mother does sums in her head continuously: 'as she drove, as she peeled potatoes, as she brushed her hair or cleaned her teeth ... Figures flew around inside her head, neat in columns, plus or minus, or jumbled and spinning, unrestrained and unstoppable.' Love-making and ironing vie for a slot as equals, with the importance of emotional life being reduced to the lowest common denominator – how long it will take.

Quality time

In recent years, the idea of 'quality time' has become fashionable. It is not *how much* time you spend with your child that counts – or so the argument goes – but the *quality* of the time that you do manage to share. Somehow this time, because it is limited and allocated its own slot in your busy day, is supposed to take on a special meaning. But, as many working mothers have discovered, children may not always choose to fit in with your best-laid plans: scheduling for quality time can backfire.

'You rush home to see the child and say, "Now we're going to sit down, or tell me everything that happened in your day,"' says Polly Toynbee. 'You put pressure on them, thinking, "I must give him some time – we're going to do three jigsaws and read three books." I will say to myself we will do something on the weekend and then he won't want to and I'll be deeply disappointed. He'll want to play with his friends rather than go to the zoo or the park. I might think it's all that time wasted.'

We talked about the child's timetable being so programmed there is no time just to 'hang out'. Polly went on, 'That's what you can't do when you're working very hard. It's hard to say, "Let's do nothing." It's "Let's do shopping" or "Let's do an activity."'

Polly is not too certain about the idea of quality time with children being something you can schedule. Time together and confidences exchanged come more haphazardly, she argues: 'You get something out of a child over a time when you're doing something together and it'll come up, not in a formal debriefing session. A conversation "happens".'

But does this mean that you always have to be available? Children have a way of needing your attention at times when you feel you cannot handle that particular conversation that they want at that particular moment. Perhaps the best way is to have a loose, overall schedule, organised enough to get things done but flexible enough for you to be able to adapt when necessary.

Deborah Owen talks of her intuitive way of responding to her family, of being 'tuned in' to what is happening. She sees the mother's rôle as 'conducting the traffic of the household. That is for me the big thing . . . you've got your finger on the pulse of the house, and if you feel that things are getting chaotic you can pick it up early and do something about it.'

In trying to 'fit it all in', so much depends on your hours of work and the place where you live. Obviously if you can go off for walks together near home without setting aside huge amounts of time, a casual stroll can be fitted in so much more often. Then there is your own emphasis and pace, and finding ways of meeting your own personal needs. What you think is important and what you are prepared to let slip all combine to produce your individual pattern. Perhaps from the different lives described here you can gain a better understanding of your own and concentrate on some aspects of your life that can replenish your resources.

Avoid worrying about whether or not you measure up to your ideals; simply do what you can. Try not to fall prey to the 'I want' syndrome and to substitute chequebook childcare for personal input, but recognise that there is more to life than simply earning a living and providing material comforts. There is the insubstantial world of ideals, principles, beliefs, spirituality, security and emotions which are strands in the web of family love that we try to weave around our children. It is this area of life more than any other which brings quality to our existence.

In her book *Stress and the Healthy Family*, Dolores Curran talks of the jigsaw puzzle of fitting children into work and life. A healthy family, she says:

> 'Communicates and listens. Quarrels, affirms and supports. Shows respect for others. Shows trust. Has a sense of play and humour. Shares responsibility. Teaches right and wrong. Has a sense of tradition. Respects the privacy of one another. Values service to others. Has family table time and conversation and admits to problems.'

It seems a tall order, but if you can say yes to some of these points you are not doing too bad a job.

What do we aim for in bringing up children?

'My children are very independent, I think, because I've always worked,' said Marion, while Joan maintained that her children were independent because she stayed home and gave them all the security they needed when small. Both women were certain that their lifestyle had resulted in children who were 'independent'.

Is independence a goal to be aimed for in childrearing today? Most of the working parents I spoke to seemed to think so. I heard success or failure measured so often in terms of whether or not a child was independent, I began to question their interpretations of the term. Does it mean that the children are self-reliant? Do they show initiative? Are they conscientious and co-operative? Or does it simply mean that they have learnt how to do without their mothers in certain areas of life?

Our use of 'independent' is as a vague term not always describing what we mean. There is a subtle hint that society wants children neatly out of the way, with all their demands and needs organised, prioritised and delegated. Employers certainly imply that they want children to be independent of their mothers who work for them. Government has whittled away child benefit effectively. Children are increasingly seen as 'making demands' rather than as people with normal human needs.

Attachment and dependence

Do we not want still to rear loving, caring 'attached' individuals rather than those who are detached and remote? There is, of course, a difference between attachment and dependence. Attachment, unlike dependence, can be expected to be a lasting social and emotional bond, keeping up a close relationship. We would like our children to grow up *attached* to their parents, but we hope they will not remain *dependent* upon us for ever.

Ignoring a toddler may eventually lead to her going off and amusing herself, and you might call this independence. But the toddler who explores from a secure base, returning often for reassurance, is the one who shows greater curiosity and will experiment more. This child will slowly grow from infancy to maturity with supportive back-up, learning to trust others and to know whom to trust. Reliance leads to a flowering *self*-reliance, that grows over time. You cannot give a nine-month-old a crash course in being independent.

Penny, who worked in an administrative post at the BBC, gave an example of one occasion when she realised that her son had developed the qualities of self-reliance and initiative: 'I was amazed, really. Tim was always rather an anxious sort of child. He used to have French coaching after school. It's quite a journey but we'd done it on a couple of weekends with him, and showed him where to go and so on. He must have been about 12. Either a bus was delayed or he'd lost his money and he took a taxi. He made the taxi go home first because he didn't have money. He explained to the taxi driver, "I don't have the money to pay you but I've got money at home. If you take me home first, I'll get it and will you then take me on to Roehampton?" And he did all that at the age of 12. I was amazed. I came back from work and heard this story and so, yes, I think they have to be more independent [when you work].'

Have children's needs really changed?

As fashions in childcare change, so do definitions. When the current vogue was that the child's needs required the mother to stay home and devote herself entirely to her, independence was seen to develop as a result of the security this provided. Nowadays, with two-thirds of mothers of young children out at work, 'independence' may be seen to grow out of a reduction of the child's needs: it often means a child who can get by on her own. Today's parents emphasise that a child needs time with other children and must be 'trained' to be independent. Some parents are saying this even before the child is a year old.

In her study of dual-career families, *The Second Shift*, Professor Arlie Hochschild, a sociologist at Berkeley, writes, 'In the earlier part of the century, children suffered over-attentiveness from the mother, now they suffer from an underestimation of their needs. Our idea of what a child needs in each case reflects what parents need.' Do working mothers wish their child's infant years away trying to make him grown-up and 'independent' too early? Is family life in danger of being marginalised in the struggle to get on in the workplace? Some suggest that a job culture has expanded at the expense of family culture.

A child-hostile world?

Roughly two-thirds of the women I spoke to said they repeatedly put family life first, but also explained that they thought society and the workplace culture made this difficult. They did not feel supported in their parenting. People expressed the idea that it is a 'child-hostile' world. They described how they kept coming up against the rigidity of the standard working day, the fixed working week and the separation of home and work which made the balancing of family life and paid work so difficult.

There was a feeling that children were being 'got out of the way' – sent to daycare, packed off to boarding school or put in the sole charge of a nanny for extremely long hours – and it was pointed out that some mothers were 'abdicating motherhood', as opposed to mothers who worked but still held on to the major rôle in their children's lives.

In reality, however, holding on is extremely difficult to do. 'Meetings where I work are always scheduled for afternoons and evenings. Corporate culture survives on a drink after work. Mothers are forever excluded from this,' says Pat. Perhaps, to survive in this environment, independence will be the most useful asset for our children.'

Judging success

Bridget, an artist, thoughtfully questioned whether 'independence' is the only measure of success in childrearing. There is 'more to it, surely. I don't think we've quite got it right.' Massage therapist Joan Stuart would agree. She feels that, 'a measure of success on this earth is a balanced individual. Help them realise that balance is what is important – an inner awareness. We are entrusted with a child. We have to consider spiritual growth, questions like, "Why are we here?" Looking at childrearing in that light, it is a protection and support to allow them to develop along their own path by providing them with food and soil to grow.'

Talking this over with Glenwyn, a BBC current affairs editor, I felt that she summed up the view succinctly when she said, 'You basically want them to emerge with their self-esteem intact.'

A subtler aim

How rewarding to be the mother of a child who, through adult life, attributes his finer sensibilities and awareness of beauty to you, like the writer Laurie Lee, or echoes your love through the years like Colette with her beloved Sido. As we rush on the treadmill of work/home/duty we find ourselves trapped in now, we may have lost the most precious commodity of mothering, time – time to be together, time to just *be*, without having to do some urgent task, without pushing the child to some educational goal, and without the TV screen as a magnet shutting out conversation.

Nostalgic for the imagined space of a bygone era, I listen to Laurie Lee reading from his *Cider with Rosie*. His mother left school at 13, worked in domestic service and then struggled to bring up a large family, not all of them her own children. Abandoned by her husband, she had the odds stacked against her. But Lee remembers her 'indestructible gaiety which welled up like a spring'. He tells us: 'She was an artist, a lifegiver, an original' who 'fed our oafish wits with steady imperceptible shocks of beauty – she was all the time building up around us, by the unconscious revelation of her loves, an interpretation of man and the natural world so unpretentious and easy that we never recognised it then, and yet so true that we never forgot it.'

Lee, that intense observer of detail, attributes his perceptive powers to his mother's example. 'Nothing now that I ever see that has the edge of gold around it, the change of a season, a jewelled bird in a bush, the eyes of orchids, water in the evening, a thistle, a picture, a poem, but my pleasure pays some brief duty to her. She tried me at times to the top of my bent, but I absorbed from birth as now I know, the whole earth through her jaunty spirit.'

What legacy will we leave our children? Is the pursuit of money, and material and career success annihilating the time and inclination to be more creative, aware and appreciative? Women worry that they may be losing their life-giving rôle in becoming bread-winners to the exclusion of all else. We need time with our children, time together to let values and dreams, inspirations and observations pass by osmosis into our children's consciousness. But time seems to be one commodity we no longer have.

Children no longer seem to have it either, as they rush from one carer to another, from one activity to another, and from computer to TV. When a mother rushes home from work to offer 'quality time' to her child she finds he is occupied, not available, perhaps, not open to the deeper conversations she, at that moment, wants to have – and has time for.

Fostering healthy independence

However, with women joining the world of work in such numbers, they are forced to place great value on their children becoming independent at the earliest possible moment. Although there are greater objectives in parenting than simply producing an independent child, I had to accept that, for many parents, this was a practical priority. How, then, can we help a child to become a balanced, independent individual? And what effect will this have on her?

John Bowlby, author of such powerful ideas as maternal deprivation in the years immediately after World War II, modified his views later and wrote, 'Evidence is accumulating that human beings of all ages are happier and able to deploy their talents to best advantage when they are confident that, standing behind them, there are one or more trusted persons who will come to their aid should difficulties arise.' This trusted person, or attachment figure, is seen as providing the companion 'with a secure base from which to operate'.

Medical author Dr Andrew Stanway believes that, 'Love, attachment and bonding are the essential building blocks for future security and the ability to form relationships.' He goes on to explain, 'Much of the anger, frustration and upsets seen in young children reflects their uncertainty about whether the parents will continue to be available.'

So, the issue is less whether we do paid work or not, than whether we are committed to the child and offer dependable responsive support. Our prime aim is that the child knows, deep down, that she comes first. In order to grow into healthy independence, it is not enough for a human being to be able to operate on his own – he needs to be able to trust others, to co-operate with them and to know how to establish and maintain rewarding relationships. All this he learns at a very young age from a consistent caring adult. If we are to foster this independence, we need to provide a springboard of love from which the child can jump that extra bit higher to reach his goal, as opposed to a ramp along which he can walk unaided, but which gives no help with the jump.

It is good news for mothers that it is not all down to us. Broadening the family nucleus to include extended family and other regular carers will not be harmful if they are responsive to the child and reliably behind her, with her parents playing the central rôle. We need to provide this consistent responsive care in one way or another. Rapid and frequent changes of carer will not encourage this. Becoming very attached to a carer and then losing this loved person is not the way to build trust.

Providing a secure base

The search is on to find dependable, responsive, trustworthy figures to help you provide your child with the secure base that she needs if she is to grow happy, healthy and self-confident. There is first of all the question of how much of yourself you want to replace. There are women who definitely do not want a mother-substitute to take their place in the lives and affections of husbands and children. In her book, *Motherhood: What It Does to Your Mind*, Jane Price argues that, 'The underlying problem revolves around a woman's sense of competition with other women.' The threat of a second mother/wife substitute in the home is a real one to absent mothers/wives, who often joke that ugliness in the carer is a main consideration in their choice.

Mothers have a need to be the most important person in their child's life – the prime carer or default carer. 'I definitely didn't want a mother substitute, so I chose a day nursery,' writes one mother. 'I paid lip service to equal sharing, but deep down I didn't want to give up so much of my share,' says another.

Eve, talking about going on tour as an actress, brought up the question of teenage problems, and leaving the decisions and discussions of issues, to a carer: 'Oh, I'd be devastated. If I were really acting thoroughly on stage and film and I'd gone off for three months to do some filming somewhere, I would hate to do that. I wouldn't mind leaving the decision to my husband, but obviously there would have had to be another woman instead of me and to leave that decision to somebody else . . .'

An inexperienced mother may fear that the carer will do such an excellent job she will 'seduce' the baby away from her. A very capable carer reinforces this mother's lack of confidence, making her feel less able to know what to do in childcare. Price says, 'Women who go out to work generally have trouble allowing themselves to be adequately replaced and these difficulties are only partially financial or practical.' Assess your own feelings, then weigh up your needs against your finances and add in any family or other help you may have, to choose what type of care you will look for. Questions of types of care are discussed in greater detail on pages 97 to 121.

The ripple effect

'. . . the aspirations and energies which might provide a tool kit from which they can choose styles of behaviour and strategies for fulfilment. This is really what a rôle model provides – not a blueprint to be copied, but an example which supplies a range of choices and possibilities, and a source of self esteem.'

Terri Apter, *The Guardian* (5.11.91)

In families where a couple of generations of working women exist as rôle models for daughters, younger generations simply take it for granted that they, too, will make a similar contribution. But images of achieving women can have a much greater influence, far beyond the immediate family; there is a ripple effect into a wider sphere than the women themselves realise. Successful women who can combine a successful working life with having a family are vitally important, for we see too many women at the top who have forgone their chance of family life.

Teenager Hannah says, 'There's no doubt in my mind that I'd never stay home full time. I plan to have a family, I'd love to have children, but I'd always feel it's such a waste – people who've gone to university or who've got something there – why don't they use it? It is possible to bring up a family and work. You're not damaging your child. Years ago that's what society thought. I don't think people think that any more. But I think if you're a working woman with a family, it's important that you keep the line that you don't put your career before your family.'

Hannah had thought it through and plans to be an interior designer with a studio at home. She feels this will enable her to combine family and career in the way that she would like. She has seen it done at first hand. Selma Hirsh, her grandmother, was social director for the Institute of Human Relations in the

USA for 40 years. 'I coped with administration, speech writing, creative programming – it was never-ending work, late at night after the children were in bed and weekends,' she says, 'but my time with the children was inviolate.'

Selma's own mother was against her working. She made it clear she would not offer any help with the children. In later life, she was to find herself living with Selma and her daughters.

Selma's daughter Donna is living and working in the UK. She teaches at the American School, she has a master's degree in educational psychology and is planning to do counselling in the next academic year. 'I think that in my own choice of profession I felt acutely that I wanted to be available to my kids during the holidays. With my degree, I really could have gone a different route. I wanted to be part of the school society and available to my kids in the afternoons.'

She explains that she wanted to be more available than her mother had been: 'I distinctly remember being 11 or 12 and not having my mother available for school occasions, but it never occurred to me that I wouldn't work, although when I first moved to England 20 years ago few women worked in this area. I think that having a professional mother at our age, in our time, when nobody else did, provided one really important thing – the realm of possibility.'

Selma's daughter and granddaughter are not the only women in the family to be affected by her. Donna talks of her cousins: 'My mother has two sisters. The younger one never worked, the older one did secretarial work when her daughter was 15. My mother was the only professional one. Between these three women they produced seven daughters. My cousins saw my mother as a keen rôle model. Every one of the seven has an advanced degree and is seriously involved in careers – doctors, lawyers, university professors. They all said that the reason they were so intent on making it work for themselves was because they felt their mothers had wasted their lives. They're constantly in touch with my mother and she is the focal point of the entire family, even after she divorced. The family used her home, her opinions, as the focus for their energies.'

Julia Neuberger can look back at her mother who worked, and at a grandmother who had headed a refugee committee, working all hours in a dedicated drive. These women make it easier for subsequent generations to assume that they, too, will do something worthwhile. Julia, in her turn, is a rôle model not only for her own daughter but, as a rabbi in a congregation for 12 years, was a vivid example of leadership and caring, of intellectual thought coupled with pastoral care.

She now works as a Fellow of the King's Fund Institute, the policy analysis institute of a health charity, examining ethics in medicine and health care. Her work involves her with medical students and, through her work with the Royal College of Nursing, she is also in contact with nurses, thus providing a model for a new generation.

Penny, whose career is described on page 50, had a working mother herself. She felt that her working had been useful to her daughters in many specific ways. She felt pleased that both girls had gone into professions: 'I think it's more important for girls to have a proper training and a profession.' She explained that when her daughter was being interviewed to get a place doing medicine, she was asked about combining work with having a family. 'She said she'd always had a working mother herself, and this was a factor in her favour.'

A new understanding

There is no doubt that seeing someone else balance family and work life has an effect. It shows what is possible, it opens new avenues to think about, broadening opportunities and lessening doubt. A group of sixth-formers I spoke to showed considerable understanding of their working mothers' needs and described how they offer support.

A number said that they spoke to their mothers about work problems and issues and offered a sympathetic ear, almost reversing the mother/child rôle. However, each one wrote in the questionnaire I gave them that they thought it was very important to tell your mother about your day after school. One or two then added, 'It is important to have *someone* there after school.'

These girls will enter the workplace with a clearer idea of what a working life involves than did many of their mothers. They will know, too, how having a working mum affects a child and what choices they will make with this in mind. They gave detailed explanations of how the needs of children varied greatly according to their age, and seemed happy now with the element of privacy they had. 'I do believe that I benefited from having *au pairs*, and thoroughly enjoyed this. Now I am older I much prefer to come home and for my mother to be at work. I simply feel pressured coming home and immediately having to enquire about my family's day. I need time to rearrange my head.'

Rôle models and the ripple effect will encourage new thinking and increased confidence, and these, in turn, will produce new expectations. If they are to be fulfilled, we need great changes in the way we structure our work and family lives.

What do parents want?

Whether I asked this question or not in interviews, these responses came flooding in. There were suggestions from people who had lived in other countries and experienced other systems, there were ideas from health visitors, childcare workers, parents and campaigners. If some of these suggestions could be carried out, working mothers, children, employers and society would all benefit.

But first the question of how involved the state becomes needs addressing. Sue Slipman, of the National Council for One Parent Families, explains: 'The challenge for government is acceptance of any rôle for the state in supporting working parents through the provision of adequate childcare and ultimately championing working practices that are more family friendly.'

Here are the suggestions that were put forward.

A new evaluation of women's and men's rôles

This would value both parents as caregivers, and would lead to a new right to leave for parents, first at the time of the birth and then in the following infant years.

Employers would recognise the responsibilities of *both* parents to their children, and childcare would no longer be the mother's realm. Regulating men's hours would promote equality.

Maternity leave improvements

Maternity leave exists but is limited by the qualifying conditions which effectively exclude a high percentage of women. Women working part time, or studying alongside work, or employed by small firms, seldom qualify. In most other EC countries, fewer restrictions hedge around this vital right. Legislation made in the 1970s was intended to provide protection against dismissal on grounds of pregnancy and the right to reinstatement during the period ending 29 weeks after the birth. It is available only to some women and the financial stress mothers find themselves under can be severe. For those who qualify, what payment there is covers only 18 weeks. There are many arguments concerning the emotional health of the mother and child which would seek to extend this for longer.

> 'Almost half of all employed pregnant women do not qualify for a statutory right to return to work following the birth of their child.'
>
> From the report 'Caring for Children' for the
> EC Childcare Network by Bronwen Cohen

Paternity leave

A statutory right for a father to take off time for the birth of a child is a popular concept among men as shown in a study by the Equal Opportunities Commission, in which 91 per cent of men were in favour of it. Fathers are frequently needed to take care of older siblings and are in practice already requesting leave for this period.

> 'The exclusion of men from any statutory entitlement to leave in relation to childbirth and childcare is preventing some men from sharing the care of their children.'
>
> From the report 'Caring for Children' for the
> EC Childcare Network by Bronwen Cohen

Parental leave

This describes leave for either parent to enable them to care for an infant. Under the Swedish parental leave system, parents are entitled to take a total of 15 month's leave in whatever form suits. One parent stays home at any time. Leave may be part time so that a worker may be kept in touch. Parents receive a benefit which is approximately 90 per cent of earnings, from an insurance scheme. A further 90 days with fixed payment follows.

In 1984, the EEC produced a draft directive outlining a possible starting point. Parents are assumed to be equally responsible for the care of their child and therefore they should be entitled to three months leave each, to be taken separately at any time in the first two years after maternity leave. An allowance would be payable from public funds. This would ensure a secure start to family life for numerous couples. Several European countries are going along this road.

Other parental leave would entitle parents to a specific number of days per year which could be claimed if a child or the normal caregiver is ill.

Out-of-work commitments of both men and women need more recognition.

> 'We should talk about working *parents*. My husband shares equally all responsibility for child and home.'
>
> A working mother

Career break schemes

Major banks and the Civil Service are offering career breaks during which workers keep in touch by working a couple of weeks each year. Re-entry schemes offer training to keep up with new developments and provide the employer with a pool of trained staff. Information packs and refresher courses are used to keep contact. Employees do not lose confidence so easily and can re-enter the workforce with ease. The employer loses fewer trained people. Because young women who envisage a career and a family will not be faced with an either/or choice, they will be attracted to such companies and are likely to offer loyalty in return.

Synchronising care and school hours with work hours

There were many suggestions about this:

- Extend the length of day in nursery schools
- Extend the age of admission in daycare centres to take infants or provide separate infant and toddler facilities
- Provide after-school care. Some boroughs do run excellent programmes using school premises, and one uses converted houses, giving a homely atmosphere
- Provide school holiday care. Holiday clubs, for example, can offer parents peace of mind and children can find companionship and wide variety of activities and outings

If working hours were shorter, and school hours adjusted, we would see fewer children coming home to an empty house. There would be fewer desperate parents cobbling together after-school arrangements with a network of different carers, any one of whom can fail.

Are extended hours at work, that keep parents away from home longer, really necessary? Many people have suggested that staff hang on at work to be seen there to demonstrate their loyalty as it is expected. Few seem to think they are really effective workers after a certain period of time. These long hours destroy family life and cannot be good for health, leaving almost no time for exercise or relaxation. Some suggested this contributed to burn-out.

'Finally the employer, if he wants to employ working mothers, must adapt. The employer must stop trying to hammer round pegs into square holes and then moaning at the poor fit, the lack of commitment, the lack of loyalty. Employers, particularly in industry, must radically rethink their employment strategies, even rethink their working practices – 9–5 are not immutable hours, they can be changed and they must be.'

Barbara Harris (respondent to *GH* questionnaire)

Childcare for all

Provision of high-quality, affordable childcare was unquestionably the most common single suggestion. The most popular form was community-based nurseries, funded by a combination of industry, local authority and parents' contributions.

Better childcare provision and parental leave would help couples make the adjustment to parenthood, would ensure children get a good start, and would go some way towards easing the dilemmas facing dual-career couples for whom the problems associated with major career interruptions and childcare problems act as a powerful disincentive to start a family. Some laughingly call these worries 'the most effective contraceptive ever'!

Making childcare a higher-status job

Value childcare workers more highly. (Childminders are unionised in Sweden and paid by local authority. Parents pay the authority on a sliding scale.) Offer ongoing consultation to caregivers, with advisors available. Professional advice could be sought by a caregiver, both for the physical and emotional health of their charges. Training and seminars would keep these workers informed and sustained.

The question of treating caregivers fairly worries mothers who are themselves asking for their rights to be recognised. Julia Neuberger said that she was unhappy with the idea of women exploiting women. (Her own nanny stayed with the family for nine years and Julia thinks this is in part due to conditions of service.)

> 'As we call for equal rights for ourselves, what about the growing group of people we employ as cleaners and nannies? There is the moral question of giving them proper conditions of service and a package of rights.'
>
> Julia Neuberger

> 'Everybody in the caring profession is underpaid in this country . . . in fact, childhood isn't valued.'
>
> Donna Geller

Regulating and inspecting childcare

Have regulated and more centralised supervision of daycare facilities that is consistent and does not fall or vary from one authority to another. Both centre and home-based care should be supervised and inspected.

Complete a resource and referral service countrywide for employers, parents and childcare providers as a partnership between employers, the public sector and voluntary organisations (like Childcare Links Brighton and R&Rs in USA).

> 'The supply side of childcare needs a revolution if industry wants to absorb large numbers of mothers to boost the flagging working population. The demand for childcare is potentially enormous and growing but mothers are responsible and deeply concerned about the quality of childcare. Whether the increase in supply comes from the private or public sector is, to a certain extent, immaterial. What is important is that childcare should not be allowed to proliferate haphazardly but should conform to a cohesive plan and must maintain strict minimum standards with a government-based regulatory body and realistic pricing.'
>
> Barbara Harris

Questions of tax

Tax relief for childcare costs, relating to nanny, *au pair*, childminder or nursery.

> 'To pay my nanny £140.00 per week I must set aside £200.00 a week as I must account for PAYE, her National Insurance contribution

and the employer's too. And this after having paid tax already on the £200.00. The real cost is £330.00 per week. Plus her food, bills, phone calls, transport, car insurance, etc. And to cap it all, I pay her Poll Tax next year! Refunding the tax I have paid on the nanny's income would have a dual benefit – encouraging more mothers to return to work and stimulating others to employ nannies.'

Nicola Catterall

'Any paid childcare ought to be tax-deductible. It's ridiculous that guide dogs are tax-deductible and this essential service is not. We seem to have equality in words, but not in fact.'

Jane Sanderson

Tax relief is offered on workplace nursery places and there is talk of extending it to all employer-sponsored childcare. It will only help some women, however.

Giving something for those who stay home with young children

A payment could be made to women or men to encourage them to stay home with very small children. (See *Parental Leave*, page 149.)

'The rôle of motherhood should not be looked upon as something second rate compared with 'real jobs' outside the home. The thought of a society where women who choose to look after their own children are looked upon as oddities is horrifying. Why should women have to deny themselves such an important part of their lives in order to be able to carry on with their careers?'

Pamela Ormerod

Less separation of work and home

There could be more flexibility about where work is done, whether in the workplace or at home. Many jobs could incorporate one or two hours in the evenings or at weekends.

'Of course people have always worked at home, not only housewives, but also writers, artists, salespeople, therapists, freelancers of all sorts and most notoriously "outworkers" employed on piecework. What's special about the homeworking practised and promoted by my own business is that it involves executive level personnel, working in services and industries that have traditionally been office-based.'

Louise Gordon

Judith Viorst injects a wry note of reality into the idea of homeworking:

I type in quadruplicate, two sets for me
And two for the baby to drool on,
In a setting conducive to grocery lists
And decisions like chopped steak or flounder?
Did Emily Dickinson have to write poems
With diaper rash ointment around her?

from 'The Writers', *People and
Other Aggravations* (1971)

Part time with full rights

We need to introduce promotion prospects for part-time employees
and nightshift workers. At the same time, we need to see acceptance
of part-time work at professional level.

'Part time is seen as a problem, difficult to adjust to, and as a favour
to the woman, this even when the alternative is that a highly skilled
professional, in a discipline where there is a shortage (engineering)
might leave.'

Caroline Gregory

'If I wanted to get on as a bright young thing in that set-up I'd
have to go on to days; there is not going to be a great deal of
promotion on shift.'

Andy (who stays on shift because of his commitment
to sharing childcare)

'I choose night duty so that if Michael is ill or is on school holidays
I am there . . . the compromise is you don't get promotion.'

Elizabeth, hospice nurse

'Part-time work is offered using dubious contract and freelance
arrangements which provide no employment benefits or promotion
prospects. These arrangements are accepted because of the difficulty
in finding alternatives and because of the effort and time needed to
fight them.

'The issue is one of labour law. It is blatantly sexist and
exploitative of working mothers. Statistics show that part-time,
low-paid, low-status jobs are done by women, part-time in particular
done by mothers. The law offers them little or no protection. Most
of the major employment laws, unfair dismissal, maternity, involve
not only a time factor but a minimum hours clause. Companies
generally don't offer pensions schemes, share option schemes and
other benefits to their part-time, low-paid, low-status staff, i.e.
mothers. I think this situation should be improved, by statute
and by a consensus in industry that these women should not be
exploited in this way.'

Barbara Harris

Personal pension schemes

'These did improve last year. If one's short-term prospects are, however, very uncertain they may not be a good buy. One may end up paying high management costs on low levels of contribution. One should be able to allocate a percentage of income to "pension" without having to buy an expensive scheme, in order to gain tax relief.'

Caroline Gregory

Making job-sharing a viable option

Only a few thousand job-shares exist in the UK, reports Bronwen Cohen in *Caring for Children*.

There have been suggestions that couples may wish to job-share, enabling a smooth handover, and offering mutual interest. Employers have been slow to offer job-sharing although, amongst those who do, it is seen that the combined energies of two people can be greater than one.

Flexitime

There is a wide variety of versions of flexitime, but the basic principle is that arrival and departure times can vary. A standard number of hours must be worked, but the exact time and regulation of these hours is flexible. Some versions demand attendance during a core period each day, while others such as maxiflex do not require this. Parents would be greatly helped by schemes like these to co-ordinate the taking and fetching of children to and from school or nursery. Rush hours might be eased and employees would be less stressed.

Within the concept of flexitime are variations such as flexiyear, in which the worker works a total number of hours in the year but may work fewer hours per week at certain times such as school holidays. All the variations offer the employee the chance to tailor her working hours to be most convenient, resulting in less stress and less absenteeism.

Providing nursery school places, state-funded, for all children

The benefit to children of pre-school education is undisputed. However, to give all children an equal start this should be available to all three- and four-year-olds.

Children's centres

The development of children's centres providing for recreational, health and social needs in addition to daycare has been suggested. These could include professional advisers for caregivers, toy libraries and facilities for special needs.

Childcare allowances or vouchers

These are offered by a number of organisations in both the UK and USA. This is practical assistance, offering the parents choice as to how they apply the money. These could be used to help pay for nanny or daycentre, childminder or nursery. There are some companies who take up places in a local or shared nursery and reserve these for their employees. In this way the employee is offered a place at a discount. Vouchers seem more popular, however, because the parent can purchase the care of her choice. Workplace nurseries are few and far between, and are not always the ideal (see page 117 for a discussion on this). But there are certain places of work – such as hospitals and educational institutions – where they can be of great value.

One or two companies are beginning to try out offering some emergency back-up childcare to employees if their own care arrangements break down suddenly. This can ensure that the worker is at work for that critical meeting even if her carer is suddenly ill. Care is supplied for a few days, and an arrangement is struck with an agency supplying high-quality trained carers.

A suitable package

In her report for the European Commission's Childcare Network, Bronwen Cohen lists some priorities, and describes a 'work and family' package:

> Given the extent of current inadequacies in provision in the UK it is extremely difficult to prioritise particular services or age groups. However, there are four issues which must be seen as central to the improvement of provision.
>
> 1   The formulation of a comprehensive policy that encompasses services, employment rights and relevant tax and social security provisions, recognises the relationship between childcare provision and equality of opportunity between women and men, and between

children themselves, and establishes a programme and targets for the improvement of provision.

2   The development of good-quality care for children under three including a programme for the expansion of nurseries, and better employment provisions for parents.

3   The recognition and development of the care functions of educational provision for children from three to 14.

4   The improvement of the pay, conditions, regulations and training of childcare workers.

There are a number of measures which could be implemented immediately. These include:

- Special financial assistance to local authorities now unable to maintain even their current childcare services.
- Providing greater recognition within the system of income and support for the childcare costs of lone parents.
- Establishing a nursery in Parliament for the use of members and employees.

A charter for childcare

The national campaign for childcare, Childcare Now!, has produced a charter of childcare. The campaign is working for the implementation of the recommendations of the European Commission's Childcare Network, which pinpointed the UK as one of Europe's most inadequate providers of childcare for working parents. In particular it wants:

- Central government co-ordination of day-care policy, earmarked public funding and a clear commitment to improve both services and employment provision
- A partnership between local authorities, employers and voluntary organisations to provide a choice of high-quality childcare provision, free or at a low cost, for pre-school and school-age children, allowing those who care for them the opportunity to work, study or participate in public life, and to give children a positive play and social experience
- Services which provide both for children's education and care within an environment which is anti-racist, anti-sexist and caters for children with special needs
- An improvement in training, pay and conditions and career structure for childcare workers, and a system of support and regulation for individual caregivers
- Improved employment conditions for all workers which would

include statutory maternity and paternity leave, parental leave, better conditions for part-time workers and time off when children are ill

Looking to the future

Women have gained footholds in the workplace, great successes in some areas and proved their worth. Perhaps the time for this proving is nearing an end. With this can come less of an aping of men's career patterns but a more flexible female shape to life. A balance needs to be found.

The early years of struggling for equality almost denied women's enjoyment of the caring rôle: 'Some women want to care, something the women's movement failed to take into account,' says Julia Neuberger. There needs to be an acceptance of the fact that people gain their comfort and satisfaction from within their families. There must be an acknowledgment of the fact that many working women will be caring for aged parents as the population takes on a top-heavy shape. This does not mean they may not need or want to work, it means the out-of-work commitments of workers have to be recognised.

We are in a transitional phase. Within memory, are traditional housewives in whom studies reported frustration and depression coupled with loss of confidence. Around us we see the superwoman model, trying to achieve at work and keep up traditional patterns at home. Women who have done this for the last 20 years or so are now saying it can't be done. You cannot do everything. There must be a change – change in society as a whole in response to the indisputable fact that women have arrived in the workplace.

In a more equitable climate, there may be fewer women with unfulfilled potential, fewer women working at jobs way below their level of training, as were those in the *Good Housekeeping* survey. Because their childcare and family responsibilities are recognised and supported they may be able to work effectively and enjoy their families. Now there is too great a gap between women's goals and reality. Julia Neuberger noticed this starkly at a school reunion. After the immense confidence of the Sixties, 'when we thought we could do anything', she found that in the Nineties her schoolmates had not all made it. Many were in 'small, part-time jobs, men had left them, they were bringing up children alone, there were financial struggles'.

This one experience of a reunion reflects the findings of the survey very accurately. We are losing the valuable contribution these women might have made with better childcare provision and greater equal opportunity. How we should value the contribution these women could make both to the family and the workplace. They should be given a full package of rights for they are showing the way to a more flexible, balanced lifestyle and should not have to sacrifice pensions rights, or training for promotion. Joanna Foster, who heads the Equal Opportunities Commission and is herself a mother of two, has written, 'What women want, and I believe what men want too, is to find a way of achieving this balance, to build into our working and family lives a quality which includes time to stay healthy and sane, time to listen, discuss, share and enjoy, time to recharge our creative batteries.'

The problems of working mothers are not those of an isolated few – they affect us all. A sensitive programme comprising education, employment, government, law, health and social services and good housing programmes can all help provide a stable and secure future of opportunity for the nation's children.

'If they had the courage to see it, the "big idea" that is staring politicians in the face is this,' writes child psychiatrist Sebastian Kraemer, 'the planned reduction of parental failure is an investment in the future of society as a whole.'

Careers list

These are the jobs done by the women who contributed to this book:

P.A./secretary
Laboratory assistant
Oil tanker first mate
Member of a collective
Furniture restorer
Plant nursery manager
Property negotiator
Accountant and worker in finance
Market researcher
Supply, special needs, part-time, full-time and hospital school
  teacher
Exhibition assistant, Eurotunnel
Librarian
Nurse
Production engineer (design)
Journalist
Actress
Solicitor
Computer systems analyst
Computer programmer
Army careers information service advisor
Deputy headteacher
Business executive
Advertising executive
Development officer, council on alcohol
Social worker
Travel consultant

Doctor
Psychiatric social worker
Civil servant
Scientific technical support officers
Production assistant
Physiotherapist
Editorial assistant
Customer services manager
Indexer of legal textbooks
Breast-screening nurse
Medical secretary and administrator
Obstetrician and gynaecologist
Executive officer, Civil Service
Locum/consultant pharmacist
Health visitor
Landlady (letting holiday cottages) and administrative bookkeeper
Senior registrar in child psychiatry
Special needs nursery nurse
Public director, Open Learning
Psychologist
Counsellor (director of own therapy centre)
Occupational therapy helper
Freelance journalist
Family planning nurse
Bank cashier
Internal auditor
Speech therapist
Social worker, juvenile justice team
Government food technologist
Child psychoanalyst
Editor of legal and banking journal
Rehabilitation officer for the visually handicapped
Advisory teacher, humanities
Supermarket shelf-packer
Operating theatre nurse
Hospice night nurse
Cellist
Illustrator
Literary agent
BBC production administrator
Company director and secretary

Deputy branch librarian
Accounts assistant
Librarian in City solicitor's firm
Law lecturer at a polytechnic
Partner in consultancy group offering courses in legal research
Childminder
Chartered accountant
Landlady
TV film producer
Author
Remedial massage therapist
Air stewardess
Shopowner
Typist at House of Lords
Information officer
Clerical administrator
Hospital administrator
Rabbi
Educational psychologist/counsellor
Architect
Social Affairs Editor BBC
Director National Council for Lone Parents

Bibliography

Books

Adam, Ruth *A Woman's Place* (1975)

Bettelheim, Bruno *A Good Enough Parent* (1988)

Bowlby, John *Childcare and the Growth of Love*, based on WHO report, *Maternal Care and Mental Health* by John Bowlby, 1952 (1953)

Brannen, Julia and Peter Moss *New Mothers at Work* (1988)

Brazelton, T. Berry *Working and Caring* (1987)

Cahill, Susan (ed.) *Mothers: Memories, Dreams and Reflections by Literary Daughters* (1988)

Curran, Dolores *Stress and the Healthy Family* (1987)

Eliot, Faith Robertson *The Family: Change or Continuity* (1986)

Formaini, Heather *Men, The Darker Continent* (1990)

Friedan, Betty *The Second Stage* (1982)

——, *It Changed My Life* (1977)

Gilligan, Carol *In a Different Voice* (1982)

Hardyment, Christina *Dream Babies* (1984)

Henriques, Nikki *Inspirational Women* (1988)

Heron, Liz *Truth, Dare or Promise* (1985)

Hewlett, Sylvia Ann *A Lesser Life: The Myth of Women's Liberation in America* (1986)

Hochschild, Arlie *The Second Shift* (1989)

Holdsworth, Angela *Out of the Doll's House* (1988)

Kozak, Marion *Day Care for Kids* (1989)

McCall, Robert *The First Three Years of Life* (1980)

Miller, Jean Baker *Towards a New Psychology of Women* (1982)

Morgan, Fidelis *A Misogynist's Sourcebook* (1989)

Mullan, Bob *Are Mothers Really Necessary?* (1987)

Neustatter, Angela *Hyenas in Petticoats* (1990)

New, Caroline and Miriam David *For the Children's Sake* (1985)

Oakley, Anne *Subject Women* (1981)

O'Brien, Patricia *Managing Two Careers* (1989)

Price, Jane *Motherhood: What It Does to Your Mind* (1988)

Pulaski, Mary Ann Spencer *Your Baby's Mind and How It Grows* (1979)

Sanger, Dr Sirgay and John Kelly *The Woman Who Works, the Patient Who Cares* (1987)

Shreve, Anita *Remaking Motherhood* (1987)

Stanway, Dr Andrew *Preparing for Life* (1988)

Steel, Maggie and Zita Thornton *Women Can Return to Work* (1988)

Stewart, Alison Clarke *Day Care* (1982)

Timms, Hilton *Emotion Pictures: The Women's Picture 1930–55* (1987)

Tizard, Barbara and Martin Hughes *Young Children Learning* (1984)

Velmans, Marianne and Sarah Litvinoff *Working Mother* (1987)

Viorst, Judith *Necessary Losses* (1986)
      People and Other Aggravations (1971)

Walkerdine, Valerie and Helen Lucey *Democracy in the Kitchen* (1989)

Winnicott, Dr W. *The Family and Individual Development* (1965)

Studies

Cohen, Bronwen *Caring for Children: services and policies for childcare and equal opportunities in the UK* (for the EC Childcare Network) (1988)

Coote, Anna, Harriet Harman and Patricia Hewitt *The Family Way: a new approach to policy making* (Institute for Public Policy Research Social Policy Paper no. 1) (1990)

Hoffman, Lois 'Maternal Employment and the Young Child', *The Minnesota Symposia on Child Psychology* (1984)

HMSO *Women and Men in Britain* (1989)

Joshi, Heather and Marie Louise Newell, *Pay Differentials and Parenthood: Analysis of Men and Women born in 1946*

Kamerman, Sheila and Cheryl D. Hayes (eds.) *Children of Working Parents: Experiences and Outcomes* (Washington DC, National Academy Press, 1977)

Knaub, Patricia Kain, *Growing Up in a Dual Career Family: The Children's Perception* (Paper for National Council on Family Relations) (1984)

Useful addresses

British Federation of University Women
Crosby Hall, Cheyne Walk, London SW3 5BA (071 352 5354)

Carer's National Association
29 Chilworth Mews, London W2 7RG (071 724 7776)

Council for the Status of Women
64 Lower Mount St, Dublin 2 (0001 615268) Represents 80 women's organisations in Ireland.

Daycare Trust National Childcare Campaign
Wesley House, 4 Wild Ct, London WC2B 5AU (071 405 5617)

Everywoman Directory
Everywoman Publishing Ltd, 34 Islington Green, London N1 8DU (071 359 5496) Annual directory of women's businesses, networks and campaigns.

Equal Opportunities Commission
Overseas House, Quay St, Manchester M3 3HN (061 833 9244)

Gingerbread
35 Wellington St, London WC2E 7BN (071 240 0953) Support group for single parents.

Kids' Clubs Network
279–281 Whitechapel Rd, London E1 1BY (071 247 3009, 071 247 4490) Out-of-school care network.

Medical Women's Federation
Tavistock House North, Tavistock Square, London WC1H 9HX (071 831 6222)

National Childbirth Trust
Alexandra House, 4 Oldham Terrace, London W3 6NH (081 992 8637 extn. 25)

National Children's Bureau
8 Wakley St, London EC1 (071 278 9441)

National Childminding Association
8 Masons Hill, Bromley, Kent BR2 9EY (081 464 6164) Enhancing status/conditions of childminders.

National Council for Civil Liberties
Women's Rights Unit, 21 Tabard St, London SE1 4LA (071 403 3888 extn. 30)

National Council for One Parent Families
255 Kentish Town Road, London NW5 2LX (071 267 1361)

National Council of Women of Great Britain
36 Danbury St, London N1 8JU (071 354 2395) National umbrella organisation.

National Out of School Alliance
Oxford House, Derbyshire St, London E2 6HG (071 739 4787)

National Women's Network
Box 110, 190 Upper St, London N1 1RQ

Network
9 Abbot Yard, 35 King St, Royston SG8 9AZ (0763 242 225)

New Ways to Work
309 Upper St, London N1 2TY (071 226 4026) Charity job-sharing and flexible working.

Pre-School Playgroups Association
61 King's Cross Rd, London WC1 9LL (071 833 0991)

Rights of Women
52–54 Featherstone St, London EC1Y 8RT (071 251 6575) Legal advice/assistance for women.

Single Parent Action Network
14 Robertson Rd, Eastville, Bristol BS5 6JY (0272 514 231)

The 300 Group
36–37 Charterhouse Square, London EC1M 6EA (071 600 2390) Campaign for women in Parliament and public life.

Women into Business
32 Smith Square, London SW1 3HH

Women in Management
64 Marryat Rd, London SW19 5BN (081 944 6332)

Women into Public Life
110 Riverview Gardens, London SW13 9RA (081 748 1427) Maintains a data base with information on women for those making public appointments.

Women Working Worldwide
Box 92, 190 Upper St, London N1 1RQ. International networking and public education.

Women's National Commission
Room 50A/4, Government Offices, Horse Guards Rd, London SW1P 3AL (071 270 5903) Advisory body to government.

Working for Childcare
77 Holloway Rd, London N7 8JZ (071 700 0281)

Working Mother's Association
77 Holloway Rd, London N7 8JZ (071 700 5771)

Index